RISE UP

Revive Your Passion
Live Your Mission

Zachary B. Michael

DEDICATION

This book is dedicated to every student who is ready to RISEUP, have their passion revived, and live on mission for the Gospel. Every generation has had a moment of spiritual awakening, and I believe we are on the verge of another because of your willingness to have God breathe in you a fresh wind of passionate obedience! This book is dedicated to every student who is willing to believe, share, and teach the Gospel of Jesus Christ to all people!

CONTENTS

ACKNOWLEDGMENTS

To my Heavenly Father and Gracious God: I praise God for being so AWESOME! He has taken me on an incredible journey, has given me grace along the way, and blessed me with this message to pass along.

To my wife and family: Through your prayers, many conversations, and giving me time away to research and write, I was able to deliver this message. I could not have done it without you guys,

THANK YOU and I love you so much!

To my students and church: I want to thank every single student who has come through 2020 Student Ministries. Your involvement, dedication, and journey with God has inspired this message that I believe will touch the lives of many others! I want to thank my church for all your support in seeing me complete this project, thank you!

INTRODUCING...
THE RISEUP VISION

Alright. I'm not sure how you got this book, but boy I am glad you are taking time out of your crazy life to give God an opportunity to use the words on these pages to radically change your beliefs and affections about Him. If it's okay, I want to put all my cards out on the table and let you to know exactly what I'm trying to accomplish with this book before you even dig in. By the end of this book, my prayer is that God will have revived your passion for Him so you can live on mission for the Gospel. I believe so much that God wants a generation of young people who are not just passionate about Jesus right now, but a generation that remains passionate one, five, ten, and thirty years down the road. There are so many people God wants to impact through you and it starts with having a crazy close relationship with a crazy awesome God! This book is intended to put before you truths of how awesome God is, how incredibly alive the Bible is, and how critical it is that you understand and take responsibility for your role in the Church. When God re-shapes your perspective on these three areas, I believe you will be launched on an amazing mission to spread the Gospel, and be equipped to share and teach the Gospel of Jesus.

So, whether you are a new seventh grader or a senior getting ready to graduate high school, God has something for you in this book. I am super excited to have you jump into the many hours of prayer and writing that have resulted in the book you are now holding. Along your journey you will find this image:

This indicates a PAUSE point. These points allow you to pause and creatively engage what you just read. You may want to doodle a thought, write some questions, draw images that come to mind, or just pause to discuss with a friend or leader. Please take advantage of these PAUSE points. I believe they are critical in fully engaging God's message for you in this book. Alright, are you ready to go?

CHAPTER 1
THE POWER OF PERSPECTIVE

As I write this I am standing in my single car garage typing these thoughts on my iPad, which is sitting on top of a rickety wood work bench that ended up being my first attempt at carpentry. With splotches of grey and red paint from some house projects, this bench accomplishes its purpose: to hold random boards and my iPad as I write. Yup, that's me, a young guy with beginner carpentry skills, a house, a young family, and a love for God and His Kingdom. This love for God and His Kingdom and His ways has been shaped and re-shaped over the years. Most recently this love has been shaped with a stronger rhythm for the Church, the group of people that share a common faith in Jesus Christ. More specifically, I have been burdened for the young generation growing up in the Church. God has called me to be a voice that points your generation back to holy and perfect God who created you and has called you to passionately live on mission for the Gospel!

The Message is Clear

My burden is found in Ephesians 5:14-16, "*Wake up, sleeper, rise from the dead, and Christ will shine on you. Be very careful, then, how you live—not as unwise but as wise, making the most of every opportunity, because the days are evil.*" You see, I believe many Christian young people have allowed the darkness of this world to dampen the passion of the Gospel. It's my conviction that to live passionately on mission for the Gospel you must re-discover your awe of God, be equipped to engage the alive Word of God, and rediscover your purpose in the Church. Why has God laid this on my heart? I believe a lot of us have hit cruise control. We start cruising away from God and more into the world. The line of right living before God slowly fades into this question, "Am I a good enough person to earn God's love?" Satan slowly drags people away in the great deception that they are their own judges; they are entitled to rule their own existence. We end up with morally good, entitled, sleeping Christians.

Think about it for a second. When you want to sleep well you shut the lights off, right? You create an environment that is perfect for optimum slumbering. Satan wants to turn the lights down on your spiritual passion so you become incapable of sharing the burning hot message of the Gospel! He wants to spread darkness to increasingly blind the souls to the glory and awe of God! My passion is to proclaim the Glory of Christ and His light and see you RISEUP from any spiritual slumber you may be experiencing. I want you to gain a fresh experience with God that will drastically change the course of your life. There are lost souls at stake that Satan is currently deceiving and it's time Christ revives your soul so you can live on mission for the Gospel!

It's time Christ revives your soul so you can live on mission for the Gospel!

As we wrap up this first chapter, I hope you have gotten a better idea of my heart and why I committed hundreds of hours to writing this book. This change in perspective isn't an easy one. I knew starting out on this project that I was getting into areas of spirituality that only God can truly change. You know what's amazing? Even with God ready to do awesome things in our lives, if our perspective is off, we will constantly be looking for the very thing that is standing right in front of us. Picture this: You feel a cool surface against your face. You open your eyes, and you are standing, facing a giant wall. Your nose is touching this wall and you start to feel trapped, almost claustrophobic. As the feeling grows you try pushing your way out. You push hard with both hands, but the wall doesn't move. Your heart-beat picks up and in a growing state of panic, you push harder, thinking with just a little more effort you can move that wall. Your life is starting to depend on it! Then, in the midst of your panicking efforts, from out of the corner of your eye you see a very familiar face. Your best friend walks up beside you, grabs your beat up hand, and carefully leads you backwards. You feel your heart beat slow as you follow their lead. Finally, you see it. The wall you were fighting was indeed a cement wall - a very tall and thick wall. Yet, you notice it wasn't very wide at all. In fact, as you stand back you realize you just needed to step back and see that you could have easily walked right around it.

Too often life feels like there's a big cement wall between us and God. God is calling us to come and join Him, but we are so caught up in spiritually suffocating activities that we are just fighting to survive. Our spiritual passion is barely burning and our spiritual life has turned into survival mode rather than thriving mode.

To join God in the mission of passionately sharing and teaching the Gospel we must have a great shift in our perspective. Let me tell you, I definitely needed it! It required a big change for me. Before we move on though, let's take a breather for a second before we uncover the great shift.

Remember the purpose of this image? This indicates a PAUSE point, for you to draw, write, or scribble down thoughts that help you think about what you just read. Maybe at this point you want to write some questions you have.

Alright. Let's jump into the Great Shift that God did in my life in order to have His glory revealed to me!

CHAPTER 2
THE GREAT SHIFT

Have you grown tired of the "church experience?" Have you maybe started to feel like the Church is dead? That it's not relevant to you? Has it become just another scheduled activity? Has reading the Bible just become another "good work" that you should probably do each day? Has God become another person requiring your precious time? Has He just slowly faded into all the relationships you try to manage each day?

You may need the same great shift that happened to me when I was twenty-seven. But before I share with you about that shift, let me share about my experiences growing up in the church.

I grew up as a pastor's kid (PK). I attended church every Sunday. I learned all the worship songs, heard the messages, prayed prayers, participated in the service projects, attended youth group, led small group in my youth group, attended mission trips when I was eight years old with my parents, and then helped lead a mission trip when I was in college. All of these experiences were incredibly helpful in my growth as a Christian. But, due to the sheer number of experiences I had, I started to grow tired of the "church experience." I was working as a full-time youth pastor for almost six years before God made this great shift of perspective I so desperately needed.

The first great shift I needed to have was regarding my view of God. God had become my job, not my God. Being in the church, teaching the Bible, studying the Bible, and talking about God was all a part of what I was paid to do. It had become so much a part of my routine and profession that I lost my awe of God. I had become so worried about finding my identity in ministry success that I started to hit the short wall. God used my senior pastor during a staff devotional one week to walk me backwards and see that, to be able to walk around the wall, I needed to adjust my perspective on the purpose of my life. **I needed to live passionately for the Gospel, not for advancing my agenda.** Friends, pride and selfishness snuck in and I lost sight of God's awesomeness. Over the next months I would sense God wanting me to sneak away from whatever I was doing and get to know Him. I began praying asking God to show me in His Word more about His character. For example, God's eternal nature was the first character trait I learned about. When this truth popped into my head, I opened up my Bible, looked up *eternal* in the concordance, and started to write down all the verses referencing God being eternal. I would write the verse down and summarize what it was talking about. Friends, I journaled that journey and it's amazing how much God taught me! My perspective on God truly was shifted. And, once again, my heart was focused on the awesomeness of Christ and my passion for the Gospel!

God did an incredible shift in my life of how I view Him so I can stand in awe of Him more and more. However, to do this effectively, I needed to be in the Word. This was the second great shift He made in my life.

For the longest time the Bible was the source of truth I knew I needed in my life to learn and grow in my faith. I knew that God used the scriptures to reveal Himself to His people and I sought after that, but it just wasn't clicking. Do you ever feel like that? Do you sit down to read the Bible and it just feels like words on a page? Don't worry, you're not alone. About three years ago I hit a desert in my quiet time with God. I would literally look at the pages of God's Holy Words and just think, "This means nothing to me right now." What causes this dryness to occur? Sin. There was a stretch of time in my life that really presented some major sin challenges. As I wrestled through these, my ability to marvel at the glory and majesty of God was replaced with a desperate need for just enough truth to keep on fighting the battle I was facing. The Bible became about me and what I needed and wanted. God-glorifying truths started to become dull and uninteresting. You know what is sad? I actually believed for a few moments in my life that since I was not getting what I wanted

I would stop reading it. There were times I would start my quiet time (pray and read), and it would be so dull and lifeless I would shut my Bible and move on with my day.

So, what was the turn-around? God's Word became a mystery to be revealed. God is eternal, which means He is endless. God started to reveal himself to me and all the sudden the Bible became a mystery I sought after. I was trusting and expecting God was going to reveal himself! Let me tell you, it's been incredible to not only be learning more about God's nature but seeing all the scriptures and how they work together to paint a beautiful and crazy awesome picture of God!

Here's the bottom line: Ultimately, the Bible is not about you, it's about God revealing Himself to his undeserving people. I didn't deserve to have God step into my pride and sin and reveal Himself so awesomely! Yet, He chose to and I am forever on a mission to make sure that you, as young people, are challenged to dig into the mystery of Scripture so that you too can discover the awesomeness of God and pass it onto the next generation!

The final shift that needed to happen was in my view and belief about the Church. I not only grew up in a Christian family going to a church, but I also grew up with my dad being some sort of pastor for most of my life and, therefore, was always around church people and church programming. Fast forward to my first few years of full-time ministry. I started out really liking the people in the church, but I hadn't ever developed a true Christ-like love for them. It wasn't until my encounter with God through His Word that I was shown how dark my heart had become. The pressures of the job started to become heavier and the thoughts of leaving started to develop. I didn't know it at first, but I had developed a real unhealthy attitude toward the people in the church. You could say my heart was growing somewhat bitter. God, in his great grace, took his 'holy 2 x 4' and smacked me upside the head with this truth: The Church is loved by God and, thus, I needed to love it. Notice, I didn't say "God likes the Church a lot," or "likes the people in Church." You never see in Scripture God saying He likes people because 'like' is just the cowardly form of love. I'm not talking about romantic love. I'm talking about a **deliberate decision to sacrifice oneself for the good of another. You don't have to like the person to love like that.** That was the trap I got caught up in. I stopped liking people because of how they made me feel. Yet, God reminded me that Christ died for those people. Christ loves those people and I'm included amongst them.

We all need a constant shift in perspective in these areas because so often these three areas become about us. The focus of our lives turns inward and thus God, the Bible, and Church are turned into vessels to serve us. The focus of your life needs to be constantly shifted onto Christ. Christ is the image of the invisible God. Christ is the point of the Bible. Christ is the message the Church is designed to proclaim.

The New Perspective

This shift starts by God revealing himself to you. As God reveals who He is you will naturally start having the passion-smothering layers removed so that the passion He lit inside of you will burn hot and bright! It's only in the revelation of The Perfect that we see our need for being perfected. When we accept the beauty of The Perfect and the purpose of being perfected, we can truly live each day bringing glory to God by spreading the Gospel. We need a new perspective on God and ourselves. I want to talk for a few moments about what this word *perspective* really means.

I want you to have a Gospel-perspective on your life. The word *perspective* finds its roots in the latin word *perspicere*, which means "to see through." I want you to see your life through the Gospel. Your life was designed to show others the purpose all of us have engraved on our souls, and that is to bear the image of Christ. To view our lives through the Gospel is to accept and celebrate our purpose while embracing the reality of sin and the forgiveness of God poured out in Jesus Christ. When we live in light of Christ we don't pretend we are perfect, having it all together. Instead, we rejoice in the perfection of Jesus and strive to reflect His grace, forgiveness, and joy he passes along to his people who are living in light of the Gospel.

The history of *perspicere* is steeped in an artistic mindset. If you were an artist wanting to draw a beautiful image of the Empire State Building in New York City, you must have many different perspectives on it. You must view it from many angles (or lenses) because it exists in many dimensions. You have the top of the building, the sides of the building, the corners, the edges, the windows, the people around the building, etc. If you were viewing this building on a sunny day, one side may look completely differently from the other side. You can't draw a beautifully satisfying picture of the Empire State Building by standing in front, looking it up and down and trying to imagine what the other sides look like. You have to look through the front lens, the side lens, the top lens, the environment lens, etc. in order to gain a whole perspective and thus reflect the truest form of the building.

It's all about how you perceive yourself and the world you live in. My challenge is to help you start seeing your world through the Gospel! The big question is, "HOW?" How does the Gospel become the lens by which we view everything? We get to know the God of the Gospel. I am praying that God uses the following pages to show you Himself in ways you have never experienced before. Believe me, I will not be saying anything new about God, but I trust they will be words that God has been wanting to use to unveil the glory and majesty of Himself to you in amazing ways! It's time to re-discover your awe of God!

Without the help of Google, draw the Empire State building from what you can remember.

Now, google it, and see how close you were.

CHAPTER 3
#GODIS PART 1

"God is so _____!" It's a phrase you hear a lot, but don't stop to think about often. Sometimes that blank is filled in with words of praise and other times words of anger, hate, or despise. Ultimately, it does not matter what words you use to fill in that blank. God is what Scripture reveals about Him because the Bible truthfully, completely and perfectly reflects the nature of God. You may have grown up with a basic Bible understanding of God, but now, through your experiences, your friends, your own struggles, or your family, you may have a completely different view of God.

I believe God can use one word to help reframe your perspective on his character. That word is **worthy.** God's worthiness revives our passion. The word worthy literally means *"having weight."* The person of God should carry major weight in your life because of the ways He has revealed Himself to you. By the end of this chapter, I pray God will have gained more weight in your life and you can't help but make decisions to live on mission, reflecting how worthy and glorious He is to you!

> God's worthiness revives our passion.

Let's start our discovery of God's worthiness by diving into the book of Revelation. Now, you need to know that Revelation is exactly that: a Revelation given to the apostle John, who was exiled (aka: survivor mode) on the island called Patmos. He was exiled under the great persecution that broke out against all Christians. He revealed many mysteries and messages that were to be communicated not only to churches in John's time, but also for the Church (the body of Christ) in the coming future. There were many crazy things he saw, but throughout the book we see multiple worship scenes that depicted angels and elders falling down in worship and glorification of God. If God's worthiness can make heavenly dwellers fall down and worship, how much more should we, imperfect selfish creatures, be in complete amazement of God humbling ourselves every day at the beauty and amazing worthiness of God?

Before we jump in, I want you to do something for me: BREAK YOUR TINY LITTLE BOX! All of us have a little box, about the size of a penny, but square. As Christians, or non-Christians, we need to take what we know about God, the experiences we have had, and put them in this box. That little box needs to be thrown down on the ground, stomped on, and destroyed! The purpose behind this is to destroy the potential to keep God where we are comfortable with him. Why try to tame a lion when you can gaze at a distance while it rules the animal kingdom with power and prestige? Why try confine God when we have been given the opportunity and privilege to sit at His feet and marvel at how perfectly loving and immensely powerful He is? God is way bigger than the box we try to put Him in. If we destroy that box we will be able to have our awe of God renewed and discover amazing truths about God that will stir up our love for Him and drive us to live passionately on mission for the Gospel! So, are you ready? Let's dive into who GODIS!

God is Father

"The revelation of Jesus Christ, which God gave him to show to his servants the things that must soon take place. He made it known by sending his angel to his servant." (Revelation 1:1)

Alright, you may be asking yourself, "Where is the 'Father' mentioned in this verse?" Great question! The focus of the whole Bible up to this point has been on Jesus Christ. The world was created through Christ (John 1:1), all the Old Testament prophets point to Jesus Christ (Matthew 11:3-4), Salvation comes through Jesus Christ (Romans 10:9), and He is reigning and will reign forever in God's Kingdom (Rev 11:15). However, now, we see that something was **given** to Jesus. That is a big change. It also signals that someone else is active in the great plan of redemption. Who is that someone else? God the Father. Whenever you are unsure about what a Bible verse may be saying, use the other verses around it to help clarify. In this case, we don't have a strong argument for 'God' meaning God the Father. If you look at Revelation 1:5b-6, we clearly see this verse referencing Jesus Christ, using the term "to his God and Father." It's safe to conclude that this is pointing back to the same God from whom Jesus received the revelation (1:1).

Okay, that may have been a lot for you to process. To recap, the revelation that Jesus received came from "His Father," who is God. So, in the first sentence of Revelation, we see that God is Father. Why is it important we understand this? We can't communicate the passion behind the Gospel if we don't see the role of the Father clearly. The passion, the suffering of Christ, meant a tearing away from a perfect relationship with His Father. It also shows the intense love Christ has for doing the will of His Father. Understanding God the Father means we understand the intense sacrifice that was shared in that relationship. That sacrifice led to Christ's suffering, which led to our salvation and the Good News.

Another reason it's important to understand this intense love of the Father with the Son is because of the real experience many fatherless youth have today. According to a new Pew Research Center analysis of the National Survey of Family Growth (NSFG), more than one-in-four fathers with children 18 or younger now live apart from their children.[1] That means that one-in-four students potentially have a skewed understanding of God the Father. These students may see the Father as inconsistent, selfish, hurtful, prideful, a liar, etc. However, God the Father is the most consistent, loving, and compassionate father ever! He has never lied, never left his people, and showed the greatest act of humility one can ever show: **sacrifice.** He gave up His Son to show you that He is serious about loving you no matter what.

If one in four students lives without a father, there is a high chance that you are without a father. If you are a student living apart from your father, I pray God reveals His love to you in a powerful and

---

1 "A Tale of Two Fathers,", accessed October 21, 2014,
   http://www.pewsocialtrends.org/2011/06/15/a-tale-of-two-fathers/.

intimate way. I pray that God wraps His arms around you, holds you close and reminds you that no matter what happens in this world He will never stop loving you and never stop thinking about you. Do you realize that the number of thoughts God has about you outnumbers the sands of all the seashores on earth? Check out Psalm 139, seriously, it's powerful! Whether you live with your father, or split time between your mom and dad, the love of God the Father remains constant, it doesn't change like that of human love. There is safety in His arms and peace in His presence. There is life in His words and grace in the cross. Before you try to share and teach others about the love of God the Father, you must first be able to share how you personally have experienced God as loving Father. Take some time in this journal page and express in images or words how you have experienced God as your loving Father, or maybe how you hope to experience God as Father.

This would be a good time to pause and journal this question and pray, *"God, give me a clear picture of what it means to be loved by you as my Heavenly Father."* Write down or draw whatever comes to mind.

God is Jesus Christ

"He (Jesus) is the image of the invisible God, the firstborn of all creation. For by him all things were created, in heaven and on earth, visible and invisible, whether thrones or dominions or rulers or authorities—all things were created through him and for him...For in him all the fullness of God was pleased to dwell, and through him to reconcile to himself all things, whether on earth or in heaven, making peace by the blood of his cross." (Colossians 1:15-16;19)

You may say, "Wait, Zach, this isn't Revelation!" I know. However, I cannot think of a more clear description of Jesus being God than this passage in Colossians and I want to give you the most accurate and supportive passage I can. This is the most important character trait of God because without this truth the Christian faith falls apart. It's not a surprise that people around the world and in America have accepted the truth that God exists, but they have also come to believe that there are many ways to get to God. If you, as students, get slowly rocked asleep in the sweet rhythm of relativity, the power available to you in Jesus to advance the Gospel is suppressed and you become like a child, *"..tossed to and fro by the waves and carried about by every wind of doctrine, by human cunning, by craftiness in deceitful schemes"* (Ephesians 4:14). Just because people may teeter-totter on the belief of Jesus being the only way to God, doesn't change the truth that He is the only way (John 14:6). Jesus wasn't afraid to walk into a heavily religious culture, practicing, what I call, "relational sacrifices," (making animal sacrifices to keep right relationship with God), and claim that He was the only way to meet with God. Jesus made NO sense to them. Jesus was stirring up a rebellion of people against the instituted system of beliefs. Yet their rebellion only made His case for salvation greater because they showed their pride and lost state of being even more.

A person's spiritual freedom from the bondage of sin and death is found in the blood and risen life of Jesus Christ! Yes, there are other ways out there that people believe will open the cell door to spiritual freedom, yet they are all seeking oneness with the true God. That, my friends, comes through grace and faith in Jesus Christ. The next time a friend says that they "believe in God," ask them if they believe Jesus is the Son of God. When someone asks you, "Who is God?" I hope and pray after reading this book that your first response is "Jesus Christ." Jesus is God and is the hinge on which all of Christianity rests. The Apostle Paul, in 2 Corinthians 15:14-17, says that if Christ wasn't raised from the dead, we are left with no hope, our faith is meaningless and we live in vain.

One of the greatest supports for Jesus being God, and for the Christian, faith is the legacy of people who have gone before us and gave up their lives for the truth of Jesus Christ. Check out this quote from an ancient church document called *The Letter to Diogetus,*

"Don't you see them exposed to wild beasts for the purpose of persuading them to deny the Lord, yet they are not overcomer? Don't you see that the more of them that are punished, the greater the number of the rest becomes? This does not seem to be the work of man. This is the power of God. These are the evidences of his appearance."[2]

Christians in ancient church history knew that the more they were persecuted the more people would see the true reality of God. They believed so strongly in the message of Jesus Christ, that they were willing to sacrifice their lives. By the shedding of their own blood others would hear the sweet melody of salvation ringing out, calling for their freedom in Christ!

[For adults reading, this is a good place to PAUSE and hear from your students their response to the quote above from the ancient church letter. How do they feel about the Christians' perspective on persecution? How do we as American Christians develop that same perspective?]

---

2 "Martydom Quotes from Christian History." N.p., n.d. Web. 15 Aug. 2014 http://www.christian-history.org/martyrdom-quotes.html.

God is The Holy Spirit

"On the Lord's Day I was in the Spirit, and I heard behind me a loud voice like a trumpet, which said: "Write on a scroll what you see and send it to the seven churches: to Ephesus, Smyrna, Pergamum, Thyatira, Sardis, Philadelphia and Laodicea." (Revelation 1:10-11)

Here we have the Apostle John giving some background of this revelation he received from Jesus to pass on to the seven churches. We see it's the Lord's day and he was "in the Spirit." If you guessed correctly, you guessed that "Spirit" with a capital "S" is referencing the Holy Spirit. Now, before we go any further, the Holy Spirit, the third person of Holy God, is one of the most misunderstood, ignored, and as author, speaker and pastor Francis Chan says, "forgotten God." What we (and I include myself in on this as a youth pastor) as youth pastors have done is under-emphasize the power and equally important nature of the Holy Spirit. When we say we worship God, we are saying we "willingly choose to bring glory to God the Father, Son, AND Holy Spirit." To isolate any person of the God-head (Father, Son, or Spirit) is to completely miss the beauty of the Holy God! Let's unpack for a few minutes what it means to worship God the Holy Spirit.

To understand what it means to worship the Holy Spirit you first must understand the role of the Spirit. There are many references to the role of the Spirit but we will cover just a few major ones.

Adopts. There's a reason God uses adoption to help us understand our relationship with him. Adoption is a two way street. Adoption is designed to give a healthy identity to the child being adopted and give the adoptive parents an opportunity to love and grow the child into a healthy, whole, and thriving individual. To understand how spiritual adoption works, let's check out Romans 8:15-16, *"For you did not receive the spirit of slavery to fall back into fear, but you have received the Spirit of adoption as sons, by whom we cry, 'Abba! Father!' The Spirit himself bears witness with our spirit that we are children of God."*

Thinking about adoption is difficult. As a guy born to a loving family with a mom, dad, and older sister, adoption is something foreign to me. Yet, when I look at my relationship with God, it becomes more clear because I know clearly the "spirit of slavery" and "fear" that Romans talks about.

When you think of slavery, what images pop into your head? What movies and what stories pop into your head? To enslave somebody is to take their freedom of choice away. My friends, sin is the greatest slave master of them all. Even Satan himself was enslaved because of the SIN he committed in wanting to overthrow God. You know what the crazy part is? We are all born slaves. We are all born with a sin nature that rules our hearts and minds. This ugly slave master shows itself in the form of selfishness. We are constantly looking to please ourselves. Yet, to live passionately for the Gospel means living to please God.

This adoption makes it possible to please God. Pleasing God is only possible because of the work of the adoptive God. God made it possible to give His children their true identity back. You see, our true identity was given to us by God, with the purpose of reflecting God in everything. Yet, the sin nature informs us that our identity must be focused on SELF. When God became man in the form of Jesus, perfectly living under the fiery temptations of the sin nature, and got up on the cross, He, in a moment's time in history, destroyed the identity of SELF! The original identity was restored! When Christ rose up from the grave in power and glory we were given the opportunity to be adopted back into our original purpose; to reflect the glorious image of God!

So, if Jesus makes it possible to have your original identity restored, what is the role of the Holy Spirit in making your adoption happen? He applies the power of Jesus in your heart and mind. He is the 'signed papers' sealing your adoption. He applies the saving grace of Jesus on your life! He is the one that helps you believe, that helps you cry out "Abba, Father, save me, free me!" The Holy Spirit reminds us constantly of our new identity. We are children of God, not children of the darkness (Colossians 1:12-14). No more do we reside in darkness when we are children of God. The Holy Spirit is working on your behalf to fight off the lies of unworthiness when you mess up. He is the truth that says, "No matter what, you are a child of God and loved completely!" Isn't the Holy Spirit awesome!?

Take some time to PAUSE and journal your feelings around the role of the Holy Spirit. Feel free to praise God the Holy Spirit for the role he has in your adoption as a child of God!

Convicts (John 16:7-11). *"You Christians are so judgmental and unaccepting of people!"* Have you ever heard that before? You see, as students living passionately on mission for the Gospel, it's not your job to convict your friends or lost people of sin. The Holy Spirit empowers you to do two things in this area: (1) lovingly confront a fellow believer stuck in sin and (2) share and teach the Gospel to lost friends. In both of those roles the Gospel is the power that births genuine change. If you have ever had to pull weeds with your parents in a garden, you know that pulling the top of the weeds off will only make them look gone for a while. Give it awhile, and they are right back there ready to be pulled again. To fully uproot a weed you need to grab its root.

The Gospel gets to the root of our heart issues every time. It's the only truth that can be proclaimed into a person's life that will save their souls from eternal damnation and cause them to start living according to God's purposes. If you are a Christian you bear the truth of the Gospel in your very body, your very soul. It's your job to share it and teach it. It's the Holy Spirit's job to use it to convict the lost souls of their lost-ness and failure to believe in Jesus.

Teaches (John 16:7-11). The Holy Spirit continues to teach the world of Jesus and His Word. The Holy Spirit inspired the 44 authors of the Bible to write down the message of God. To this day, He is the source that makes this ancient text come alive (Hebrews 4:12). I believe whole-heartedly that before we can passionately live for the Gospel we must have our hearts torn up by God's Word. We must have our souls pierced by His truth and taught what is right so we can see and know and confess what we are doing wrong. It's pretty amazing that God not only inspires a book that has persevered over the centuries but continues to strike the hearts of those who read it; that is simply amazing! All this is done through the power of the Holy Spirit. So, when you want to understand a Bible passage, ask the Holy Spirit to teach you. When you want to be able to teach someone else a biblical truth, ask the Holy Spirit to teach you. He is your spiritual teacher. Seek him out!

Judges (John 16:7-11). Alright. We don't like this word. But, here it is, the Holy Spirit judges. He brings the absolute right-standards of living that God has set forward and holds people accountable to. He is God's "mobile judge." The Holy Spirit roams the earth as the source of God's truth to humanity. When He decides to hold someone accountable to God's standards, that person will be fully aware of their standing before God. In most cases, He will use us to communicate absolute truth. 2 Corinthians 5:17 says He makes His appeal to men, through us. So, empowered by the Holy Spirit, are you willing to be a voice of absolute truth in a world ruled by relativity? I can guarantee you will be looked down upon, hated upon, and called stupid and narrow-minded. But what is your mission? Will you please the world or passionately live for the Gospel? Gospel living Christians are voices for God's absolute truth that will be used to judge the world and hold them accountable to God's absolute standards.

Helps you pray (Romans 8:26-27). Finally, the Spirit helps us pray. Do you ever struggle with that? Do you feel like you are taught you SHOULD pray but struggle with what a "good prayer" life looks like? Don't worry, you're not alone! So, whether you are a 13 year-old just starting to really wrestle with believing in God, a 16 year-old who is pretty confident, or an 18 year-old ready to launch into college life, there's a constant truth that we can rely on to help guide our prayer life: the Holy Spirit. Check out what Romans 8:26-27 has to say:

"Likewise, the Spirit helps us in our weakness. For we do not know what to pray for as we ought, but the Spirit himself intercedes for us with groaning too deep for words. And he who searches hearts knows what is the mind of the Spirit, because the Spirit intercedes for the saints according to the will of God."

First off, it's okay to acknowledge weakness. It's okay to say, "I'm not the best at praying." If we can admit we are weak at praying it opens up the door of our hearts for the Spirit to come in and help us pray awesomely! The Spirit **helps** us, and it's okay to need help. If we want to live passionately spreading the Gospel, we must allow the Spirit to work as He desires and that means allowing Him to help us pray.

How does He help you pray? Have you ever had a friend who was hurting, and needed prayer, but you had no idea what to pray, so you didn't? These are the moments where God, the Holy Spirit, is ready to help you pray. When you are in those moments of being unsure about what to pray, in your heart, ask the Holy Spirit, "Holy Spirit, please help me!" When you are asking the Holy Spirit to function in His biblical role, He will fulfill it, He will help you! Learning to trust the Holy Spirit takes time, thus it's critical you set aside time to pray, learning to listen to the Spirit, so you can know what He is saying. If you can discipline yourself to spend time talking and listening to God in prayer, you will find your passion continually fueled and your mission consistently clear and motivating.

Why can we rely on the Holy Spirit to help us pray? *He seeks to accomplish the will of God.* You see, the Holy Spirit does not act outside of God's will because, remember, He is GOD! Therefore, if we are seeking God's direction on something we can be confident we will receive a clear and true answer because the Spirit knows and accomplishes the will of God (1 Corinthians 2:11-12).

Friends, the Spirit knows the deep things of God, the will of God. We can be confident that God, in His free gift of the Spirit, will help us pray prayers that seek to accomplish His will.

CHAPTER 4
#GODIS PART 2

In the first section, we broke down the essence of God, His triune, three in one nature. We learned that God exists in the persons of Father, Son, and Holy Spirit. It's okay if you still have a lot of questions about what we call the Trinity. It's not meant to be understood. It's like asking my two year old son Eli to understand algebra, no way! He understands the most basic commands we give him ("don't touch the ornaments on the Christmas tree," "don't hit," "eat your food," etc.). We can expect him to understand those commands, but anything more complex and abstract, no way.

God cannot be fully comprehended by our tiny human brains, and that's okay. He is the greatest unsolved mystery while, at the same time, the most fantastic mystery ever revealed! He has revealed parts of who He is through the alive Word, the Bible. That, my friends, is what I want to do now. I want to lay before you captivating pictures of His awesomeness as revealed in the book of Revelation. May His Word capture your heart, stir your affections, and remove the dark cloud of the world that may be blinding you to the majesty of our God!

God Is Holy

"Each of the four living creatures had six wings and was covered with eyes all around, even under its wings. Day and night they never stop saying: 'Holy, holy, holy is the Lord God Almighty, who was, and is, and is to come.'" (Revelation 4:8)

"When I started high school I was starting to get my life together. I had a group of friends that I was really close to. None of us believed in God. But when I started coming to church and learning about how real God is, I was amazed at His grace and love for us and got baptized. My friends thought I was strange but let it go.

Soon enough, they would start making jokes about Christianity and were confused when I defended the validity of it. They thought I was strange for actually believing in God. Little by little they stopped including me and thought I was a crazy, naïve, 'Jesus freak.' Even my best friend of ten years thought I was crazy. I worked on stopping the bad things I had been doing before. That isolated me further from them. Eventually, I realized that my faith in God was more important than being friends with them, and I realized that if God was calling me to let go of my friendships with them, then I would have to do it. After I started distancing myself from them a little my best friend stopped talking to me altogether and told many others at my school not to talk to me either. It was hard and I didn't know what to do. The verse I kept coming back to at that point was Philippians 3:7-8, "But whatever were gains to me I now consider loss for the sake of Christ. What is more, I consider everything a loss because of the surpassing worth of knowing Christ Jesus my Lord, for whose sake I have lost all things" (NIV).

God is so much better than anything we have in this world. He calls us to put everything second to Him, because He deserves our worship. And, I have to say, although I do miss the friends I lost, what I gained was so much more valuable."

-Fiona, Graduated Senior from South Nassau, NY.

I start this section on God's holiness with this story because it is a perfect example of what happens when you truly encounter God's holiness: separation. Can you imagine such an intense experience with God that it causes you to walk away from your friends, even your best friends? We need to ask the question, "What does our life look like when we are struck by God's holiness?"

Humility. When we put ourselves in front of God's holy and set apart nature we are struck with humility. Those angelic beings constantly declared how awesome God is. There wasn't an ounce of pride in them. They realized how small and helpless they were in the presence of God's holy presence! The culture you and I live in does not foster humility, but pride. Selfies, Snapchat, and social media are the lush fruits of a generation focused on self. Was this the intent, to create a self-centered culture? No. Am I calling everyone who uses social media self-centered? No. I am saying that we are so easily lost in self that we lose what it means to walk humbly. To live in a vibrant relationship with God we must daily focus on God's holiness so we continually receive and walk in humility.

Hope. In its basic understanding holiness means to be "set apart." God is supernaturally set apart from us. He is outside of time and space. His reality includes our reality, while at the same time includes all of history, our future, and all eternity. You can say God is preparing tomorrow because He is already there. He is set apart from every limitation; He is limit-less. When we start to live in the reality of God's holiness, His set-apartness, we gain huge confidence in his ability to do great things! Nothing is too big for Him because He causes mountains to rise and fall. He can bring wind, fire, and hail to our planet and yet not be impacted because He is the originator who is outside of His creation. He is not moved or shaken by the brokenness we experience first-hand. You see, it doesn't matter what you lose or suffer, it matters who you are in relationship with. For Fiona, it meant being so devoted to God that losing friends wasn't about losing friends, it was about gaining a relationship with all-powerful, all-knowing, and all-loving God! God's holiness must be the factor that separates us from the rest of the world. Because when the world tries to destroy our lives, we will have an outside source that is un-moveable, a rock we can build our lives on! As we depend on God as our source of hope we are the living hope the world so desperately needs!

God is our true north. God's holiness is not only our hope in life, it is our spiritual compass. A compass always points to true north. You could say it's absolutely right. When we come into contact with God's absolute rightness we find the direction we are looking for. Whether you believe fully in God, or you are still asking questions about God, I challenge you to consider the true claims of God as expressed in scripture. I believe God's absolute right standard of living offers the most complete and fulfilling direction for our lives. My life makes sense because God is holy. Your life can make sense if you believe that God is holy. We were created to live in righteous obedience, doing the will of God to reflect the holy nature of God to everyone we come in contact with. People are seeking for the truth, and when we live in the truth of God we live set apart, and our passion is revived and we live on mission for the Gospel.

[For adults reading, this is a good place to PAUSE and hear from your students their response to Fiona's story. Can they relate? How? Do they agree with Fiona's decision to lose friendship over God? Why? Why not?]

God is Creator

"You are worthy, our Lord and God, to receive glory and honor and power, for you created all things, and by your will they were created, and have their being." (Revelation 4:11)

Let's think about the human body for a minute. The human heart is able to pump about 1,850 gallons of blood every day in your body; 660,430 gallons of blood are pumped every year; and 52,834,410 gallons of blood are pumped for a person who lives to be about 80 years old.[3] Your heart is an amazing muscle created by God to do extraordinary things! That is just one piece of your human body that God created. Don't even get me started on your brain. Your brain is made up of around 100 billion (100,000,000,000) neurons that act as the whole control center for your body[4]. The complexity of our bodies is purposeful: to reveal the glory and majesty of God as our creator! Not only has God directly revealed Himself and His glory through human beings, He has shown Himself majestic and glorious through the created world.

When was the last time you thought about what generates our earth's ozone layer? Well, let me help you out. There is a unique natural lightning phenomenon which takes place in Venezuela. It is a cloud to cloud lightning occurrence that generates about a three-mile voltage arc (that is 15,840 feet). This happens when winds from the Andes Mountains collide with ionized gas coming from marshes. This magnificent storm can be seen from up to 250 miles away. This storm is constantly active. It actually acts as a light that guides ships in the dark.[5] God not only spent detailed time crafting you and I, He set up the world we live in to self-sustain and shield us from the burning hot rays beaming from the sun. If it wasn't for the ozone layer, humanity would not be able to exist.

What lasting, daily impact does this have on your life? You are growing up in a culture that has deemed the scientific theory as the basis for identifying objective truth. Yet it seems as though science itself is starting to struggle with its claims of God not being our Creator. Check out this quote from Tim Folger, an author for *Discover* magazine, one of the most popular read science magazines:

"Its basic properties are uncannily suited for life. Tweak the laws of physics in just about any way and—in this universe, anyway—life as we know it would not exist. Consider just two possible changes. Atoms consist of protons, neutrons, and electrons. If those protons

---

3 "Heart Facts,", accessed August 15th, 2014,
   http://upbeatheartsupport.org.uk/medical_matters/heart_facts.html.

4 "Nervous System,", accessed September 19th, 2014,
   http://www.innerbody.com/image/nervov.html#full-description.

5 "7 Natural Phenomenons You've Never Seen.," Oddee.com,
   November 06, 2007, oddee.com/item_91568.aspx.

were just 0.2 percent more massive than they actually are, they would be unstable and would decay into simpler particles. Atoms wouldn't exist; neither would we. If gravity were slightly more powerful, the consequences would be nearly as grave. A beefed-up gravitational force would compress stars more tightly, making them smaller, hotter, and denser. Rather than surviving for billions of years, stars would burn through their fuel in a few million years, sputtering out long before life had a chance to evolve."[6]

I hope your jaw dropped a little bit after reading that quote because it is simply amazing how the world of science continues to get rejected by the very natural world in which they worship. Tim Folger, the author of this quote, labels himself as a naturalist. If you claim to be a naturalist, you believe the physical realm is all that exists. If it can be tested, measured, and objectively studied, then it's real. Therefore, anything outside the natural realm does not exist, including any possibility of a supreme being (God). Literally everything we know in the universe would not exist if it hadn't been so extremely fine-tuned for the existence of the human race. There is a creator behind everything we see, smell, taste, hear, and touch. He has not only revealed himself in the written Word (Bible), but in the very creation we are blessed to exist within every day (Romans 1:19-20). Those who claim there is no God because you cannot prove him are sadly in need of you who are passionate about sharing the truth of God's awesomeness and equipped with the knowledge to have meaningful discussions that lead to passionate followers of Jesus Christ.

God is Overcomer

"Worthy are you to take the scroll and to open its seals, for you were slain, and by your blood you ransomed people for God from every tribe and language and people and nation, and you have made them a kingdom and priests to our God, and they shall reign on the earth." (Revelation 5:9-10)

---

6   Tim Folger, "Science's Alternative to an Intelligent Creator: The Multiverse Theory," DiscoverMagazine, December 2008, 1, accessed March 14, 2014, http://discovermagazine.com/2008/dec/10-sciences-alternative-to-an-intelligent-creator#.UyN2gdy1TfA.

Christ was slain. Have you ever thought about Christ being slain, murdered, or killed? He willingly gave himself as a sacrifice that required a brutal killing. Your salvation came because an innocent man allowed himself to be killed at the hands of murderers. I don't know about you, but whenever I see an injustice or have an injustice done to me, I get furious. When we watch movies that have an underdog we always pull for the underdog, right? I remember watching the movie *42*. It was released in 2013 and tells the story of Jackie Robinson, the first African-American player in Major League Baseball. He overcame great obstacles and injustices to become one of the greatest baseball players who has ever played the game. When I watched that movie I sat there getting mad at the ridiculous amounts of racial prejudice and injustice that was driven by sinful, wrong, and unjust social standards. There is something deep down within us that identifies with the underdog, with the helpless; those who have the odds against them but somehow they overcome. We want to overcome.

We are helpless before God. The odds are not in our favor and we are the underdog. Yet, Christ, who became helpless, having the odds stacked up against Him, overcame. He is our overcomer. He has ransomed us from our helpless guilty standing before God. When Satan tries to tell us that we are good for nothing hypocrites who don't deserve victory and who will always fail, WE OVERCOME. The powerful truth I want you to believe is that no matter what you are facing, Christ HAS overcome it! Satan has no power to hold you down, Christ has OVERCOME!

Better news yet, not only does Christ help us become innocent and victorious, but we become "priests" and collectively a "kingdom." We are exalted to a state of existence that has great responsibility and authority. The underdog wins again, and this time the underdog rules all! Reviving your passion means walking in power and authority over temptation, laziness, complacency, and forces of darkness. Don't think you are some incapable weak Christian. Christ has overcome, and therefore you are empowered to overcome and rule with Him!

Pause for a moment to write or draw any sin(s) you struggle with that need to be overcome and defeated. Draw or write the sin, and then draw an image showing Christ defeating it. Ask God to help you believe in His complete and overcoming work on the cross!

God is Just

"Just are you, O Holy One, who is and who was, for you brought these judgments. For they have shed the blood of saints and prophets, and you have given them blood to drink. It is what they deserve!" (Revelation 16:5-6).

Too often our perspective on God gets drawn into the love, mercy, compassion, and forgiveness of God. While those are equally powerful and critical to experience, we tend to lose sight of God's just side. It's in His justice that He simultaneously acts as our overcomer and as our judge. He holds up His standard of righteous living and punishes those who fail to live up to it. As revived and passionate Christians, we must not minimize for a second the just nature of God and the life-changing impact He can have on us. Throughout Scripture God is seen as a just judge. He doesn't allow the standard He has set for his people to be lowered at all. We must always remember that the standards He has set before us in the Bible flow directly from His nature. The very same nature that demonstrates unconditional love also demonstrates unconditional rightness. Yet we live in a world that is filled with conditional relationships, right? Our whole lives are immersed in conditions. Let's look at one example:

Teams. I remember my 8th grade year very well. In this period of my life I went on a very life-changing mission trip to the central city of New Orleans. I was very involved in my youth group and I was finally part of the big "8th grade group" that everyone in the school anticipated being a part of. However, the most important aspect of my 8th grade year was basketball. It was specifically focused on whether or not I was going to make the A-team or B-team. Maybe you know the feeling. The infamous try-outs take place and you work hard. You are hoping the coaches didn't see those few mistakes you made. You are super nice to the coaches. And, you are putting forth extra effort to be nice with your "teammates," which, in that setting, are really your arch enemies who are fighting tooth and nail for that same glorious membership on the "A-team." Well, the tryouts finally arrived. I put forth my best effort as a straggly 8th grade boy and, somehow, I made the team. Yes, the A-team! It felt good to make the team. I had met the **conditions** placed forth on me by the coaches who had decided there was a certain standard that needed to be met in order for us to make the A-team.

We live in a conditional world, but we're created to be unconditionally loved by God. That's a hard adjustment! It's tough because the conditions God has set for us to live up to was fulfilled in another person. It would be like me making the A-team on the basis of another player greater than myself. Each one of us wants to earn our spot in anything we do, it gives us a sense of pride, accomplishment, and purpose. Yet God goes against all natural laws and grounds His unconditional love in the work, merit, and skills of Jesus Christ. You are loved by God because God decided to love you through Christ. The only way a sinful human is to experience the love of God is by accepting humbly the work of Jesus in their place, acknowledging that **they aren't good enough.** God's just character exists to remind us that we are not good enough, that we need Jesus!

God's just character forces us to consider every day our shortcomings in view of God's perfection. We are forced to consider, "If God is perfect, and he demands perfection, I know I fall short and something needs to be done, daily." Daily, God wants to remind you that you are in relationship with the most perfect, powerful, and loving person ever! He wants you seeing how awesome he is so you can get lost in that awesomeness! As you lose yourself in God, you are driven to confess your wrongdoing because you care more about remaining in God's presence than living apart from Him in disobedience.

GODIS. I want you to remember that before the world, GODIS. Throughout our entire lives into eternity, GODIS. We will never come to point of knowing the whole character of God, but what we do know is enough to center us on our need for the Gospel and equip us to live in accordance with His will. The character of God is our source of passionate, Gospel-centered, living!

CHAPTER 5
THE GOSPEL

"The man called his wife's name Eve, because she was the mother of all the living. And the LORD God made for Adam and for his wife garments of skins and clothed them." (Genesis 3:20).

Echoes of Eden

If you are reading this, and have grown up in the church, or been around youth groups a few times, you have probably heard the story of how Adam and Eve disobeyed and were given consequences. One of those being that their eyes were opened to the shame of their nakedness. What did they try to do? Cover up, of course! They pulled together some leaves and tried to hide their nakedness from each other and God. Yet, all their attempts failed and therefore God, in His great love, made the first declaration of Good News by killing some animals and using their skins to cover Adam and Eve. The Good News at that moment was no more feelings of shame because they were covered up.

When we spring forward thousands of years we hear the very clear echo of the Garden Good News when the Lamb of God, who takes away the sins of the world, is sacrificed on the cross of redemption[7] and glory. In the moments of the Resurrection the trumpets are unleashed and the victory song of the Lamb is proclaimed in the heavens! Because of the resurrection of Jesus, anyone who confesses with their mouth "Jesus is Lord," and believes in his or her heart that Jesus in fact rose from the dead, will receive the covering of God in Jesus Christ! The shame that our sin brings, that doubt that runs

---

7   "Redemption"-To be saved from the judgment of God on all sin"

rampant in our unbelieving hearts, is put to death when the blood of the Lamb is poured over our hearts and we receive new life! And that, my friends, is Good News. That is the Gospel.

But what specifically does this mean for you and me in our every day lives? I want to present to you a section of Scripture that captures the essence of the Gospel yet causes much hardship and confusion.

"As for you, you were dead in your transgressions and sins, in which you used to live when you followed the ways of this world and of the ruler of the kingdom of the air, the spirit who is now at work in those who are disobedient." (Ephesians 2:1-2)

Paul, the author of this letter to the believers in the church of Ephesus, is making specific statements to the lifestyles "pre" and "post" Christ. If you notice, Paul uses the word "were" to mark a clear difference in lifestyles. He does that to help them realize how drastic a change the Good News of Jesus really can make. He goes into describing their "pre-Christ" condition of living, and it's *not* good. It reminds me a little of the show *Walking Dead*. Yeah, you know the show I'm talking about. If you don't, it's about a man in search of his family in a land that is surrounded by the "walking dead." He must learn new ways to live in this reality with his two friends who are there to teach him and help him survive.

Why this example? Well, for starters, **death remains alive.** The whole show is based around a family being sought out in the midst of alive corpses who were once dead. In Paul's description of their "pre-Christ" life, death remained alive. The death Paul was referring to is solely defined in "transgressions and sins." How do we know what sin is? Well, God has given us the law. The Israelite people had a law to live by and we too have a law to live by. As Michael Horton states, *"The law still cannot produce in me the desire to keep it; it can only tell me what God requires."*[8] Take a minute and look up Romans 3:19-20 to get an even a better definition for the purpose of the law.

Not only is the law a clear description of what God requires, but

8 Michael Horton, Christless Christianity: the Alternative Gospel of the American Church by Michael Horton (Jun 1 2012) (Ada, MI: Baker Books, 1001),

what God requires is so high that we will never be able to obtain it. Thus, we fail and we fall into sin. We understand what sin is when we understand the law. The law does have a purpose in our lives—to remind us of our inabilities to fulfill the expectations of God, to *"Be holy as I am holy"* (1 Peter 1:16). How is it possible to become holy as God is holy when there's no possible way anyone could ever fulfill the commands to the upmost perfection that God requires? That was the trouble with the Pharisees in Jesus' time. They believed perfect obedience to the law meant the highest level of spiritual maturity. Jesus came and dashed that belief system to pieces when He made the work of God more about the heart than the actions. So, our transgressions and sins become known to us when we stand in front of a Holy God and allow His Word to expose the filthy rags of righteousness that we try to bring before him. At one time we were walking around dead in the belief that our good works, our righteous acts, somehow merited the favor of God. Where's the Good News?

"But God, being rich in mercy, because of the great love with which he loved us, even when we were dead in our trespasses, made us alive together with Christ--by grace you have been saved--and raised us up with him and seated us with him in the heavenly places in Christ Jesus." (Ephesians 2:4-7)

The Gospel is a mirror we need every day to see the reality of who we are without Christ - the walking dead. Yet, in God's great love and mercy He makes us alive, pouring out His grace to those who believe through faith in the Good News of Jesus Christ. My passion is to see God raise up a Spirit-filled army of believers, an army who has been awakened by the Gospel, with the light of Christ shining in their hearts so all may be exposed to the great love and mercy of God! God has done something like this before in the past. Check out Ezekiel 37:1-10. Read this slowly, imagine the scene!

Notice something. These dry bones didn't do anything to gain this life. They can't boast in their new life, it was given by God! God shows great mercy and grace so that no one may boast about how great of a Christian they think they are. Even if you read your Bible every day for the rest of your life, it doesn't give you one-second to think somehow you have earned God's saving life. God, rich in mercy, poured it out on you and I. We were flat-out broken sinners. THAT IS GOOD NEWS!

What is the Gospel? It is the constant reminder of Christ's perfection covering your imperfection. It is the constant challenge we face to receive the free gifts of mercy and love as we struggle to believe we are worth such marvelous gifts. The Gospel will put us in uncomfortable places and call us to believe things that seem scandalous but are really genuine loving affections flowing down from our holy and loving God.

Christ lives within you when you profess faith in Him. When you are able to believe that reality your life will start to see some major changes. You will start wanting to share this good news with others and teach this good news amongst friends. It is critical to embrace this mission to share the Gospel to all people because the more we embrace it, the harder we can fight to say yes to sharing the Gospel, the stronger we stand against a driving force that I know first hand can attempt to suffocate your passion for seeing others experience the love of Jesus.

Turn the page to hear more.

CHAPTER 6
THE BATTLE OF FEAR

Little did I know that fear would be one slave master that I would allow to put shackles on my heart.

Growing up I was the kid that always wanted to do the right thing. For example, in the small Christian school I attended everyone knew you were a trouble maker if you got a yellow slip. When I was in 8th grade I crossed over. Yes, during one of our breaks I had gotten into the classroom 30 seconds late which was enough to receive the dreaded yellow slip. For me, it was a sign of humiliation. I was becoming the guy I never wanted to be. The worst part of it all is that they had to call my parents. Oh man, my parents were the last people I wanted to let down. I begged the teacher to just look over my offense and let it go because I didn't want to lose the respect of my peers or disappoint my parents.

That fear, as innocent and stupid as it sounds, took root in me. It started to grow over time and it came out again when I dated my first real girlfriend. That's when IT happened. You know - "IT" - the relationship defining conversation to end all conversations. I was going off for a 10 week internship to Central City, New Orleans, to serve alongside Urban Impact Ministries.[9] Knowing our relationship was serious enough that we would head towards tying the knot after I got back, my girlfriend wanted a commitment before I left her behind. As a high school student, not really knowing myself or what I wanted, I got really scared. I was overwhelmed with all the insecurities of our relationship. We pressed on though through the summer. When I got back and the fall semester started we had "IT."

---

9 www.urbanimpact.org

I shared why I didn't feel she was the right one for me. Let's just say my reasons were like sharp arrows that pierced her heart and tore her apart. She was left broken into a thousand pieces. In that moment, I thought I knew why I was breaking up with her. But, I was just scared, fearful of commitment, and fearful of making the biggest mistake of my life. After that moment of heartbreak I vowed I never wanted to hurt anyone like that again. This was all based and rooted in fear.

That fear grew and grew over the years. When I met my wife I subconsciously approached the relationship out of fear. I made sure I was doing everything possible to not hurt her or make the wrong decisions. You know how crazy that drove her? It has taken years of God's grace through our marriage to help me finally realize how much fear has controlled me. It not only crippled my ability to be confident in who God has created me to be, but also crippled our ability to build trust.

Friends, fear is a very powerful reality. That's why the Bible speaks about how fear is not designed to be a part of your passionate, Gospel-centered life. God did not create you to fear, to cower in the dark, or to be passive. We see multiple passages of Scripture dealing with fear. Do you know why? **Fear is a barrier to passionate, sacrificial, Gospel living.** We see this in many Scripture passages throughout the Bible. Let's check out a few.

Joshua 1:9 (Look it up!)

This verse takes place right after Moses, the great leader of the Israelite people, has passed away. God raised up a guy named Joshua to take his place. The transfer of leadership and power is significant.

Joshua not only had to fill big shoes, but he had a huge task ahead. God didn't just tell Joshua to not be a scaredy cat, He says to him, "look to Me, YHWH, the I AM because I AM is with you wherever you go." God offered Himself to Joshua. Joshua has the unlimited source of power, wisdom, and everything he needed to be obedient to wherever God called him to be. God left Joshua with no excuse to not move forward in faith.

Fear masks itself as a safe place to exist while actually crippling your ability to demonstrate Godly faith and live dangerously in God's will. You wanna play it safe? Live in fear. You wanna live how God wants you living? Live by faith in Jesus. When we live fearlessly obeying God's call we are living passionately for the Gospel. We start making the priorities of God the first priorities in our life. When living this way we don't care anymore what people think. If you quit a sports team because you are making God your priority - don't be afraid, do it! The only person you are created to please is God. God will bless your decision to live fearlessly and to follow whatever it is He is wanting you to do. We see this promise show up in Isaiah 41:10.

> **The only person you are created to please is God**

Isaiah 41:10 (Look it up!)

When we believe in our hearts that God is trustworthy and that He is with us, we receive strength that holds us up and gives us a steadfast spirit to remain faithful to Him. God is calling His people in this passage to keep their eyes on Him. He is reminding them that, "Hey, I chose you, I called you to myself. When all these nations around you threaten to harm you, fear not, focus on me! I've got you!" God has your back when your faith is in Jesus Christ. God doesn't call you to live safely, He calls you to live passionately. He gives you everything you need to live a life that embodies and exudes the sacrificial, passionate life of Jesus!

Here are a few questions you have to stop and ask at this point: *Why are you afraid?* Why does what people think about you scare you? Are you afraid to let your parents or best friend down? What makes you afraid to turn down watching a filthy comedy if it means losing "cool points" with your friends? Do you find it hard to trust God?

> **God doesn't call you to live safely, He calls you to live passionately.**

2 Timothy 1:7

"For God did not give us a spirit of fear, but of power, love and self-control." We were never created to experience an emotion that causes us to hide from other people or from God. Yet, when we gaze back into the Garden, we see the source of the fear we experience today. When Adam and Eve decided to not trust God, they sinned. When disobedience entered creation so did shame and fear (Genesis 3:8-10). Their disobedience turned God's "very good" created order into a place of hiding and shame. We are ashamed, we don't want others to see the true us, so we hide behind things. You make sure you have the trendy clothes and the trendy gadgets. You never invite friends over because they may discover your parents are on the brink of divorce. You know you are really not that smart in a class, so to impress a certain group of friends you cheat on tests to get good grades. You feel so alone in this world that even though you are surrounded by hundreds of people at school, and even though you have 1000+ friends on Facebook, you withdraw and hide in the grips of pornography, cutting, binging and throwing up, not eating, and contemplation of suicide. This is all because you don't feel like anybody truly accepts you for you and that there is something so shameful about you that no real person could truly accept you for you.

My friends, God did not put that spirit within you. That spirit you hear telling you how worthless and shameful your life is—that is the spirit of Satan himself, the great deceiver. You know why I know that? I know that God did not give us a spirit of fear, but of **power, love, and self-control.**

You are created in Christ Jesus to live with a spirit of power, courage, and boldness! You are created to be bold and live confidently. This is not because of your good works, but the good work of Jesus Christ on the cross! When we live confidently in Jesus we live passionately for the Gospel. Satan does not want you feeling confident about your life, but instead to be always doubting, questioning, and wondering what people think of you. God has done something amazing to free you of that fear, shame, and guilt. He has given you a spirit that testifies to the **love** that is shown to you by God.

There isn't a person on earth who loves you as much as God does. It is critical that at some point you genuinely believe, because if we want to live fearless we must live in the acceptance of God's perfect love, "For His perfect love drives out all fear" (1 John 4:18). What makes God's love so perfect is the complete surrender of Jesus to His Father's will. Jesus loved His Father so much that even after asking for a way out, He bowed his knees, bowed His spirit, and gave up life. Jesus did not have His life taken from Him. Jesus laid it down willingly (John 10:17-18). True love is not taken, it is given away, no matter if you like the person or not. True love is free from conditions. Jesus had every right to keep His life and retain His glory and majesty of being God. The next time you think you're a good person and that God owes you something, think about what God did and allow humility to sweep over you like a flood. God's love is something we will never understand, but it is there for us to receive. For those of you who have a relationship with Jesus Christ, you have the Holy Spirit that reminds you every day of God's love for you. He reminds you of the great love act that was shown to redeem you from the pit of hell. Fear tries to keep you isolated and unloved, but God, through Jesus Christ, has come to love you and set you free! Now, the big question remains, what happens when we are free? What happens when we start living out from the overflow of God's divine love? We live a Spirit-filled life fueled by power and free of fear!

Passion fueled by power. *"For God gave us a spirit not of fear but of power and love and self-control"* (2 Timothy 1:7). Now, I realize I just mentioned this verse above, but I want to refocus us on it. This time I want to focus on the "power and self-control" aspect. If we want to continually live out of the overflow of God's love, we must make a Spirit-empowered decision to trust God's love. Why is that important? Because **other people need to experience the love of God!** John 13:35 says, *"Your love for one another will prove to the world that you are my disciples."*[10] If we want to passionately spread the Gospel, the love message of God for the world, we must live lives of godly love! And that, my friends, starts with the Holy Spirit.

10 New Living Translation.

Self Control. In Galatians 5:23 it says a fruit of the Holy Spirit is "self-control." When we live in the life of Christ we walk by the Spirit of Christ. There are whole books devoted to the study and understanding of the Holy Spirit, but in this brief section I want you to focus on the fact that you, as a believer in Jesus, have been given the Spirit that does not shy away. Nor is He weak, but instead He is made up of POWER! To love people the way God loves requires a super-natural power that does not exist inside a normal human being. Check this out: the word used for "power" communicates *"inherent power, capability of anything, ability to perform anything, not merely capable of action, but power in action."*[11] When you receive Christ you inherently (through the nature of Christ) receive this power to not just have capabilities to take action, but actually DO what God wants. You have the ability to love people even when you may not like them! You see, the Spirit knows the deep things of God and therefore will empower you to literally go love the unlovable, because if God has chosen to love you, a sinner like the rest, He for sure wants others to experience the same thing!

At this point let's pause and ask, "Do I trust the love of God enough to live fearless for God?" You were not created to live in fear. You were created to be loved by God so you can love other people with God's love.

All this is good and as a young person I was in your shoes. I heard all this, believed it, and little did I know, fear was growing and gaining control. I have now, many years later, pinpointed areas of my life that only strengthened the spirit of fear that battles with the spirit of love and power. What are some areas in your life that increase fear and weakens your ability to trust and love? Take a moment to pause and journal any thoughts you may have so far. Feel free to draw images that represent anything that causes fear in your life.

---

11 "Bible Gt (Great Treasures),", accessed July 30, 2014, https://greattreasures.org/gnt/main.do.

Write prayers to God asking Him to help you trust His Spirit to live confidently for Jesus! This is your space to think through how fear has played a role in your life and how God is wanting to remove it!

CHAPTER 7
THE ALIVE WORD

It is the all-time best seller. Argued to be one of the most stolen books of all time. Contains a highly contested message. Claims absolute truth. You guessed it; The Bible. It lays claim to all of those descriptions. The Bible isn't just a book that a Christian should read. It's a widely debated, historical, and scientific document that gives headaches to those in the fields trying to disprove or prove the certainty of its claims. To start off this chapter, before we jump into the power of God's Word and how can learn to share and teach it effectively, let's build a foundation. Let's get to know some real places, real people and real experiences that are found in the Bible and in real human history.

The Validity of Scripture

Real places. *(1) Consider ancient Bethlehem, the birthplace of Jesus.* Bethlehem isn't just a historical city, but a divinely appointed place in God's supreme redemption plan. To show the validity of this location God allowed archaeologists to discover an ancient artifact called a *bulla.* A *bulla,* was used *"to seal an ancient shipment of a tax payment to Jerusalem during the First Temple period of the kings."*[12] From this finding God has given his people a real confirmation of the historical validity for the birth city of His only Son Jesus Christ. *(2) Trial location of Jesus.* In Jerusalem you can now visit the exact area where Jesus was held on trial right before His crucifixion. We are finding more and more historical evidences for the life of Jesus

---

12 "Artifact Confirms Ancient Bethlehem." N.p., n.d. Web. 15 Aug. 2014.
    http://www.icr.org/article/6891/310/.

and this gives us more reason to believe the claims of the Bible.[13]

Real people. Ever heard of King Hazael? Well, if you cracked open your Bible to 2 Kings 12:17-18, you would discover that Israel had been threatened by the Syrian King Hazael. King Hazael was on a war path (just having took over the city of Gath, and set his sights on Jerusalem). All freaked out, Joash, King of Judah, pays off King Hazael with all the gold and gifts stored up in the Temple of the Lord. This act of fear is considered a victory for Hazael because he comes away a much richer king and showed his dominance as a conquering king. What's amazing is that in 1993, at the site of Tel Dan in northern Israel, there was found a recording of the victory that King Hazael had over the nation of Israel and the "king of the house of David" in the ninth century BCE.[14] King Hazael was not just a King described in the Bible, but a real, scientifically confirmed, ancient King that supports the claims of Scripture!

Real experiences. The island of Patmos is where the Apostle John was exiled and where he wrote the book of Revelation (Revelation 1:9). Now, at the very surface, if you just google "Island of Patmos" you will find many current references to the island still known as Patmos today. So thousands of years have passed and to this day, the island that once held John, still exists. Getting to our real experience however, we must look at the backdrop to the book of Revelation. In this backdrop we find a massive persecution of Christians carried out by many Roman rulers including the famous ruler, Nero. If you want to read a more secular account describing the events to the backdrop of Revelation check out the Bibliography at the back of the book for a link to Tacitus (the history book of the Roman Empire).[15]

I pray your faith in the credibility and believability of Scripture has been enormously expanded. I pray now we can openly hear the truth

---

13 "Archaeologists Say They've Uncovered the Site Where Jesus Was Tried,", accessed January 7, 2015, http://www.relevantmagazine.com/slices/ archaeologists-say-theyve-uncovered-site-where-jesus-was-tried.

14 "The Bible Unearthed,", accessed January 29, 2015, https://www.nytimes.com/books/first/f/finkelstein-bible.html.

15 "Tacitus: Annals Book 15,", accessed November 3rd, 2014, http://www.sacred-texts.com/cla/tac/a15040.htm.

of Scripture so God can stir a great hunger inside each of us for His Alive Word! Let's unpack for a few minutes why it's important to radically pursue the message of Scripture.

The Alive Word is a huge source of passion!

You need to engage God's Word with reckless abandon. If you didn't know where your next meal came from you would be constantly on the look-out for food, recklessly trying to figure out what you will eat next. If we view God's Word as "optional" for our spiritual passion, rather than required, we will always live a life of apathy and complacency rather than passion and purpose! We will get too comfy in the world and slowly start to let our guards down and be carried away by the soothing call of the world. It can't be optional to be in His Word because God's Word is alive, it's active, (Hebrews 4:12) not stale!

> If we view God's Word as "optional" for our spiritual passion, rather than required, we will always live a life of apathy and complacency rather than passion and purpose!

When we come to the Word with expectation of encountering Him He will meet us and we will leave different. Are you satisfied with where you are? Are you scared that maybe somehow God's Word will show you something that will force you to abandon your old ways and embrace something new, something immensely larger than yourself, out of your control and completely and indefinitely out of your comfort zone? In this case, if you stay in the spiritual comfort zone, you are making a decision to ignore the awesome presence of God. I'm sorry, but that fear is not a good enough excuse to NOT engage the living Word of God. I can't decide for you how passionately and zealously you will engage God's Word, but I can only speak from experience that the more I engage God's Word, the more I'm hungry for it. It's just like your physical appetite. When your body needs nutrients, it will send hunger pains. When your brain interprets those signals and you understand that you're hungry, you eat. Every time you feed yourself when you're hungry you become stronger, healthier, and more stable.

I have been working with students in grades 7-12 for over 7 years now and something I have learned is that *passion determines priority. What you hunger for is what you will seek to fill your life with.* I have seen students so passionate about certain activities that their passion to live for the Gospel would take second or sometimes third or fourth priority. I'm sorry to break the news to you, but your passion for God doesn't grow unless you are exposing yourself to His holiness on a daily basis. When you approach God's Word with expectation God will fuel your passion for Him!

God's Way of Relating

The second reason it is so critical we recklessly pursue after God's Word is because God has revealed Himself in the written Word and therefore it's His way of relating to us.

Every time we open the Bible we must start by focusing on *the relationship.* At its very core the Bible is the story of God relating to humanity. The second level of that story shows the *direct relationship* God has with His people and *the desired transformation (change)* he wants His people to experience. Let's break these down for a minute.

Direct relationship. The direct relationship we see in Scripture is simply this: **The character of God in relation to the character of man.** Let me give you an example of this. The character of God in Romans 3:21-22 is "righteous." In relation to God's righteous nature we learn about the law. The Law, which is comprised of just over 600 laws, is a direct tool given to show man's desperate need of saving from *unrighteous* living. God knew the people couldn't live up to all these rules, that's why he established "relational sacrifices" (sacrifices to make their relationship right with God). When we understand the direct relationship God has with his people we start to see the transformation that comes from that relationship.

Desired change (transformation). God made a commitment to his people that He would never leave them. For a righteous, completely perfect, God to be in relationship with an imperfect, unrighteous, people He required some sort of change. That change is discovered in His righteous character which revealed that to be WITH Him we must be SAVED by Him. He saved his people through relational sacrifices. Thousands of years later His Son, Jesus Christ, made the final sacrifice declaring us righteous before our Holy God. The transformation that He desires in all of us is the transformation that comes through faith in His Son Jesus Christ. Below is a visual of the process I worked out. It's easy to remember and easy to write down on a napkin when you're out with friends or just studying on your own. A great tool to help explain how the Bible relates to our lives!

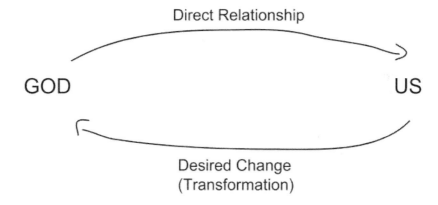

Direct Relationship

GOD   US

Desired Change
(Transformation)

Why is reading the Bible like this so critical? When you come to Scripture you are intentionally putting your focus on the source, God. Way too often, we will read a Bible passage and immediately try to find ourselves within the scriptures. We ask, how does this relate to *my* life? How does this help *me*? Remember what I said earlier; small decisions create monster habits. Every time we make a decision to look for us in any passage we create a monster habit of looking for us when we should be looking for God. If we view the Bible as a source for our betterment, happiness, or overall success the Bible will become distasteful. It will become something we dread reading because we will never find what we are looking for. We will find God in the Bible and a lot of the times he doesn't promise happiness, success, or betterment of life **in the way we are seeking.** When we seek God first, we come to accept and become passionate about what God wants. That, my friends, does not give happiness, it gives true joy. It doesn't make us successful, it gives us concrete purpose and passion; pure drive to accomplish God's purposes.

My challenge to you isn't an easy one; it's not simple. I'm asking you to crack open the Alive Word of God and not focus on yourself. Don't look for yourself. Don't ask "how does this relate to me?" Don't desperately seek a clear cut and easy answer that will somehow fix your problem. God didn't give us His Alive Word to fix our problems but to make us more holy, more set apart. I'm challenging you to enter the process of being made more like Christ. That starts by you daily giving up other time-sucking activities to sit down and allow the God of the Universe to reveal Himself to you! Passionately, recklessly, fight to make time for God to unveil the mystery of His eternal character so you may become more like Jesus and spread the name of Jesus in your everyday life!

PAUSE and I challenge you to look up these three character traits of God using biblegateway.com. Using the space here or in a separate notebook, take some time to write down what these traits reveal about God, what they show about you and what change God wants to see in your life.

1. Holy

2. Zealous/Jealous

3. Patient

CHAPTER 8
THE CHURCH: ARE YOU RELATED?

My wife, Celeste, and I have had the great blessing of receiving two beautiful children, Eli and Eliza. Eli is our two year old son and our daughter, Eliza, was just born to us on November 9th, 2014. When Eli was born, we instantly started to ask the question, "Who does he look like?" We would analyze his facial features and draw conclusions based on his face and big brown eyes. As he got older we heard a lot of "he looks like Zach" or "he looks like Celeste." Now, at almost two years of age, he has a great balance of us both.

Enter his baby sister. As I write this Eliza is one week old. She has a full head of hair (unlike her brother when he was born), pudgy cheeks, and baby blue eyes. It's pretty clear that she has her mom's eyes, her mom's cheeks, and her dad's hair. It will be fun to see her grow and morph into the beautiful young lady God has designed her to be!

Both Eli and Eliza are clearly identifiable by their parental features. You can tell who they are related to by how they look. I believe it's the same when we talk about the Church. As we enter this portion of the book, I want you to be focusing on the Church as a Family, related by the blood of Jesus Christ. To guide our thinking about the Church I offer this working definition: *"One Body, united in One Spirit, on mission to share and teach the Gospel to All People."*

If you notice, the first part is "One Body," or "the Family of God." Ephesians 5:11 explains Christ followers as "children of light." We have been transferred from the dominion of darkness into the kingdom of light (Colossians 1:13-14). You could say we all shared a similar birth mark, sin. That birth mark indicated our relationship as children of darkness. However, when we receive Christ we are transferred and made into children of light! Darkness is removed by the glory and light of Jesus! What does that mean for helping re-shape the perspective we have on the Church?

Well, in the Church we are like any family. And, just as with any family, comes fighting, division, arguments and unhappy people.

If you have at least one sibling you know what I'm talking about. You don't think the same way they do, especially if you have a sibling of the opposite gender. Let me tell you, I have an older sister. As the younger brother I knew my roll; pick on my older sister as much as possible. That naturally created arguments, but it also provided us opportunities to deal with our frustration in a healthy way. To this day, my sister and I have a fantastic relationship and it's not because we never fought, it's because we learned how to deal graciously with each other.

The Church is no different. We are one big spiritual family with Jesus Christ as our foundation. Yet, in spite of our unity, we find many divisions. It seems like our experiences, knowledge, judgments, and convictions have influenced how we understand God, the Bible, and what the Church should look like. Over the course of hundreds of years the Church has splintered into many different little "churches" like what we see today.

When you pull up Google, and search for "churches" around your area you will find many different types of churches. Here are a few of the churches you may find: Catholic, Lutheran, Evangelical Free, Evangelical Covenant, Non-denominational, Baptist, Christian and Missionary Alliance, Assembly of God, and many more. My guess is you don't care much about those titles. I bet you would check out any church as long as you have a good friend to hang out with. There's some real strengths to having this perspective on the local groups of Christians that meet together as the church. You bring a message of unity amidst diversity. You emphasize relationship over religious institution.

Your generation is unique because it is set up to change the course of how the Church functions as One Body. God has designed His

Body to operate inside relationships that give rather than take; relationships that heal rather than inflict wounds; relationships that promote truth rather than compromising doctrine; and relationships that shine a beacon of hope in a very dark world! Churches like this do exist. However, we have a lot of work to do and it's in your hands as to whether the Church grows strong in these areas or grows weaker. How do we grow these areas stronger? We keep our focus on the primary foundations of any local church. I want you to have a clear understanding on three core truths that bind the Family of God together no matter what period of history you find yourself in: (1) The Gospel, (2) The Bible, and (3) Sin and Humanity.

The Gospel

God wants a crazy close relationship with you, even as an imperfect person. In His great love, He has offered His son as the perfect way for us to enter into this relationship. We must confess we are sinful before God and believe that Jesus walked a perfect life, died with the sin of the world on the cross, and rose again overcoming the power of sin and death! From this confession and belief in Jesus, we are filled with passion for the lost, poor and needy. The Gospel becomes the lens from which we see and live our life. In short, the Gospel is: Christ crucified, Christ resurrection, repent, believe and go share.

The Bible

A church must believe in the *inspired, inerrant, and infallible Word of God.* Let me unpack these quickly.

Inspired. The Bible was inspired by the Holy Spirit and penned by human hands. God decided to use the minds He had created to pen the very truths that shape the faith we hold to so strongly today.

Inerrant. The Bible is "without error." The original documents penned by the authors are called "autographs." These autographs were completely inerrant. However, over time, these original autographs disappeared. But we have copies that were made by Christians. Today we have enough of the copies, and fragments of the copies, to piece together the original message of the autographs penned thousands of years ago. Let me just get something out on the table right away. The Bible contains small errors such as spelling discrepancies. However, none of these errors change the main message of the Bible!

Infallible. Simply put, the Bible is believed to be the absolute truth and revelation of God for all humanity. It is the absolute standard by which God holds humans accountable.

My encouragement to you is this: be on the lookout for churches that hold to inerrant and infallible views of Scripture. These churches are the ones you will see around for a lifetime and be vibrant in their ministry. Why? Because they have not shifted with the popular beliefs of culture. They will have stayed firm to the claims of the Bible and that will make them shine even brighter for longer, and reach more people than ever!

Sin and Humanity

Lastly, I want to make sure you realize how important the teaching on sin is for a person attending church. Here's the bottom line: all people are created in God's image yet born into sin (Genesis 1:26-27, Romans 5:12-13). You and I were born to reflect God, but we received a nature from Adam and Eve that wants nothing to do with God. We bear the image of God, but we also contain a nature that rebels constantly. Never let church teach you that you are by nature, "good." Yes, we are able to do "nice" and "good" things but so is a high percentage of the world's population. God doesn't care how "nice" of a person you are. He cares that you are made right by Jesus Christ! You need to be a part of a church that teaches you and reminds you of your natural standing before God (sinner), and then your right standing before God (when saved by Christ). The moment you start believing you are "good," your "goodness" starts to muddle with the belief of being righteous and all that does is make you equally responsible for your salvation. Did you hang on a cross brutally beaten and marred beyond human recognition? I didn't think so. Make sure your church is teaching truth about the nature of humanity in light of Jesus Christ.

Being able to identify the proper beliefs of a church is the first step in understanding what a true Bible believing church family looks like. Right behind that is seeing how a close family treats each other and relates to one another. We could reference a lot of examples of what healthy relationships look like within the body of Christ. I want to narrow in on one group of people that I believe we, as the younger generation, need to start loving better. The elderly.

The elderly population were once the builders, working away shaping and molding the Church. Now, however, they are the bedrock, the rich heritage that shapes many churches and gives strong direction. If you want to have a positive and effective impact on your church, while living passionately for the Gospel, then get to know the heritage by spending time with the elderly. Here is a Scripture to get our minds focused on the importance of this relationship:

"Are you the first man ever born? Were you brought forth before the hills? Do you listen in on God's council? Do you have a monopoly on wisdom? What do you know that we do not know? What insights do you have that we do not have? The gray-haired and the aged are on our side, men even older than your father." (Job 15:7-10)

If you know anything about the man named Job, you know he is always the poster boy for learning how to find God's purpose in suffering. Although that is absolutely true, we find other life-altering truths embedded in the story of Job that relates to you, me, and to all JR/SR high students in the Church.

As I write this two celebrities recently passed away, comedians Joan Rivers (81 years old) and Robin Williams (62 years old). Although neither were your typical "elderly" who live in an assisted living home, they are old enough and famous enough to make me stop and think about their lives. When they died they left behind a legacy. They left an imprint on humanity that will never be lost. However, they also left behind fortunes and fame. The reality is that no matter who you are, we must all face the pending grips of death and no amount of wealth will impact your life after death.

For you to live the mission God has for you, you must have consistent interaction with the elderly because the elderly give us the **right and true perspective on life and the church.** When we slow down enough to think about the life of an elderly person, we find that they have actually lived a long life; they weren't just born that way. Let this sink in. At age 80, an elderly person has lived almost five times as long as the average reader of this book. Let's say the average reader of this book is 16. That means an elderly person at the age of 80 has lived your life five times over. They have five times the experience, five times the wisdom, five times the hardships, five times the fun, five times everything! That's why this passage in Job is so critical to believe and understand. As a young person living in a culture that worships youthfulness, you must reject the worship given to you (as empowering as that is) and focus on the elderly. Focus on their wisdom, experience, and the rich history that they represent. If you want a true, honest, and clear perspective on life and the church, seek the wisdom and experience of an elder, not the youth praised by culture. When we focus primarily on youth, we start to blur out the older and elderly of the group. We miss out on the rich heritage and their deep rooted convictions that have shaped our churches. Elderly need to be celebrated, appreciated, and drawn upon by you - the developing leaders of the Church NOW. You are in the process of shaping how the Church will look in years to come. The Gospel is to be reflected in **all people**, and thus we must not throw aside the elderly and their rich heritage that exists in our churches. Be the generation that embraces the heritage, celebrates the elderly, demonstrates godly love, and seeks godly wisdom as you develop into servant leaders.

My challenge to you, as it relates to living as part of the body of Christ, the Church, is to take time in the next week to identify just one elderly person who you can get to know. I'm not asking you to dedicate tons of time to hanging out playing Rummy or Hearts. I'm asking you to start off by dedicating small portions of time just talking with them at your church. Ask them about their grandkids. Ask them about their favorite memory of being in high school or Junior High. Ask them if they served in a war. Ask them to tell war stories. Just ask. That's what I did with my Grandpa, Grandpa Wink.

Grandpa Wink served in WWII and fought in Okinawa. His team was tasked with taking out a Japanese sniper. While in route my grandpa was shot in the shoulder. He survived the shot and was award the Purple Heart for his service. As young kids he would always show us his battle scar and we would have him tell the story over and over again. It was thrilling for us to hear the experiences of his past and, little did we know, it informed our future.

In the last 6-8 years, I have visited my Grandpa in Texas and have gotten to hear all sorts of stories (both from War and from life). I have seen and held old war bullets, old Japanese money, and yes, I even held his Purple heart in my own hands. To this day I try and call my grandpa pretty consistently just to check in and see how he is doing.

You know what the bottom line is for you? Care for the elderly. Show them you are different than any other young person who they sometimes literally "bump" into. Show them you will stop to help them pick up the comb, purse, or handkerchief that they may have dropped. Don't just stop there though, ask them how their day is and if they need any help shopping. Stop by the house down the road where you know an elderly person lives. See if they have a favorite cookie or bar you can make them. Write them a note each week telling them you are praying for them. In doing all this you are telling people with your life that you believe the elderly have wisdom and are worth your time, energy, and resources. You are telling people that God cares about the shut-ins and those who have lost their spouse of 50 years. And, you are willing to be the person or the youth group who lives to be the Gospel displaying the sacrificial love of Jesus Christ to these people.

Everyone needs each other to grow because each has a unique perspective on life that clarifies the fogginess we settle into. Keeping and living out of this perspective is difficult. That's why we are bonded together in "One Spirit."

CHAPTER 9
THE CHURCH: PART 2 – ONE SPIRIT

"There is one body and one Spirit—just as you were called to the one hope that belongs to your call." (Ephesians 4:4)

Yes, we are talking about the Holy Spirit that we covered earlier on in the book. Not only does the Holy Spirit teach, convict, judge, and help us pray, He is also the glue that keeps the Family of God together in all circumstances. He helps us grow from living together with each other by helping us learn the strengths and weaknesses of one another so we can become as effective as possible in sharing and teaching the Gospel. Scripture says we all have a role in this family and the way we love one another is by living out these roles amongst each other. These roles are found in Romans 12:3-8, check out the passage and then read on.

This passage is in the context of loving God and doing His will, which includes living in love as members of God's family. We do this by asking God to help us see the gift He has given us and then actually going out and doing it. As we live out our gifts we demonstrate the grace and love needed to thrive together as the Family of God, young and old people alike!

These are what we call "gifts of the Spirit." Why? The Spirit binding the Church together enables the family members of God to practice their gifts in order to demonstrate God's love to each other and to those outside the church. Please make sure you understand this opening truth: **we exercise our spiritual gifts in the amount of faith given to us by God.** That means that ultimately, we don't decide our spiritual gifts or how well we are able to practice them. God has given us faith to exercise these gifts at the level He has set.

Therefore, you may not have the spiritual gift of abundantly giving, but you may have the gift of encouragement and you use that gift to the full, not worrying about other people's gifts. The most powerful picture of Christ known to the world is the one painted by the brush strokes of God's children as they live to love as their Father has gifted them. Our gifts are given to demonstrate the Gospel of Christ and, therefore, we must not get into competition with each other. To further understand all this, let's take a moment to break this passage down.

Multiple Gifts

All gifts are equal in value. You are not any more special than the person next to you in church. God has given you each an equally valuable gift to exercise. It even says *"don't think more highly of yourself than you ought"* (v3). Just because you may have the gift of teaching, doesn't mean God values your input or prayers more than a person who cleans up after the toddlers during Sunday morning nursery time. I want you to check yourself; check your heart. If you are feeling frustrated with not feeling like you are valued in the church, or that your gifts are not valued, check your heart to see if you are over-valuing yourself.

> The most powerful picture of Christ known to the world is the one painted by the brush strokes of God's children as they live to love as their Father has gifted them.

Prophecy. Some people have the gift of prophecy. Now, is this "end times prophecy," or "fortune telling power"? No. What has been revealed about the end times is captured in the book of Revelation. Only God is all knowing and can know the future. However, what this gift does mean is God has given some people a sensitivity and ability to understand and communicate the will of God *as revealed in Scripture* for a person or group of people. Acts 21:10-11 tells of a prophet who predicts how the Apostle Paul will be imprisoned for Christ. The purpose of a prophetic predication is not solely to tell the future, but specifically lay out the will of God for a person or people with the intent of calling them to greater faith in God. In this case, the prophet was revealing God's will for Paul and we see (a) the faith of Paul and (b) the faith of the people. Paul responds in great faith to God's will and the people who were initially fearful for Paul, release their doubts and respond with, "Let the will of the Lord be done." All over the Old Testament the prophets are given messages which predicted future events that call God's people to display a greater faith in God.

To summarize, the gift of prophecy is given to a person who speaks the very Words of God with the intent of building up the faith of the individual or group that it intends to reach. Every Word must align with Scripture otherwise the "prophet" shall be considered false and be rejected.

[Take a few moments to discuss your understanding of prophecy and consider any questions you may now have before reading this chapter. If you believe you have the gift of prophecy, I would highly encourage you to share with your parent, your youth leader, youth pastor, or someone who can help you discern and validate this gift].

Service. Some people just have a heart inclined to serve. They find much joy and purpose in working hard behind the scenes to make other people successful. I struggled with serving for a long time. I knew it was good to do, but personally I would have rather spent time doing something entertaining rather than serve. Ever been there with me? Are we terrible Christians if we struggle with wanting to serve? Yes. JUST KIDDING! I am making sure you are still with me. We aren't terrible Christians, but we may want to check our hearts and see who we are really wanting to please, ourselves or God? Now, some people have the spiritual gift of serving, others don't, and that's okay. However, those who don't have the gift of serving are not let off the hook. They must seek God's face even more to be given an open and compassionate heart to serve. (Okay. Right now I want you to google "Tim Hawkins Servants Heart video." Click on the video that is about 50 seconds long, hilarious!).

Teaching. This means you have an ability to help others understand truths related to the Gospel. This gift does not mean you should become a school teacher. Your school teachers are educated and gifted in communicating and teaching academics. To teach means you have a Spirit-filled ability to understand the truths of the Gospel in a way that allows you to communicate them to others and help them believe and live out the Gospel. This may mean you become a minister or a pastor. However you also could be gifted to sit across a table and help friend (s) understand God's truth in a way that really connects with their life.

Exhortation. Exhortation is the gift of presenting the truth of Jesus in such a way that it calls for a specific response of action. Practical example? Preaching. However, don't think this is a power-trip for pastors or preachers. Another way to understand this gift is "encouragement." In the same sentence, the original Greek language uses variations of the word *paraklēsis* to communicate this gift as "a calling to one's side, a calling near."[16] In Ephesians 4:15 there is a very clear example of what a person with the gift of exhortation will look like, *"Rather, speaking the truth in love, we are to grow up in every way into him who is the head, into Christ."* A person with the gift of exhortation is gifted in speaking God's truth **in love**, with the intent to see the person or people grow more into the image of Christ. Let's not mistake "love" with a "soft, pat on the back, everything will be okay because you keep sinning" type of love. It's a sacrificial love that is willing to speak the truth on behalf of the best interest of the other person. This comes from a desire to see them grow into a clearer image of Christ.

Giving. The Spiritual gift here is focused not on the AMOUNT of what a person gives, but on the generosity of the gift. It's focus is on the heart of the giver. God doesn't want a stingy giver, but a person who opens their hands to however much it is God wants them to share. Whether you are giving your money, time, or skills, God cares more about the attitude of your heart in giving than how much time

---

16 "Bible Gt (Great Treasures),", accessed November 1, 2014,
     http://greattreasures.org/gnt/main.do

you spend, or how much money you donate. I want to make sure we draw a distinction between a non-Christian who gives lots of money and a Christian who has the spiritual gift of giving generously. A philanthropist is a wealthy person who gives their money and time to better the lives of people. A Christian, with the spiritual gift of generous giving, has been blessed with a greater portion of faith in being able to give generously to the will of God for advancing the Kingdom of God.

Leading. What is the first image that pops into your head when you think of leadership? Maybe it's a quote like this from President Ronald Reagan, *"The greatest leader is not necessarily the one who does the greatest things. He is the one that gets the people to do the greatest things."*[17] Maybe you think of your sports team and you picture the outspoken, highly talented captains who lead the team? Do you ever picture a leader who is soft spoken and working behind the scenes? There are so many different types of people who demonstrate the ability to lead people to accomplish a common goal. However, the Spiritual Gift of leadership is different from these because this gift is given to individuals who will provide spiritual direction to a group of people seeking God's will. God doesn't care if you are super popular or super shy. When God gifts you in this area, He has decided to use YOU to lead people into the center of His will. If at all possible, tear away from all the culturally stamped ideas of what a true leader looks like. Remember, our goal here at RISEUP is to re-shape your perspective on who God is, the role of the Bible and Church in your life.

It is crucial that you understand the role you have as a member of God's family. It cannot be shaped by the world but rather by God's Word. In 1 Samuel 16:7 God specifically identifies what He cares about the most in a leader, *"Do not look on his appearance or on the height of his stature, because I have rejected him. For the LORD sees not as man sees: man looks on the outward appearance, but the LORD looks at the heart."* You may have heard this verse before, but it is so true! David is being chosen in this verse to be anointed as King of Israel and everyone was looking for the guy whose appearance fit

---

17 "Short Inspirational Student Leadership Quotes,", accessed November 3, 2014, http://studentleadership.com/short-inspirational-quotes/.

what everyone culturally expected a King to look like - tall, strong, warrior-like, authoritative, etc. However, God rejects that image and says, "No, I will use a shepherd boy to lead my mighty nation." David may not have demonstrated a physical strength that people were looking for, but he demonstrated a strength of character that God cared about the most. The character of a person is an overflow of the condition of their heart. The Spiritual gift of leadership has to do with the condition of a person's heart. The spiritual leader's heart is willing to completely surrender to God's will. This is critical because if they are to lead other people into the center of God's will, they themselves must already be passionately abiding in that very will! God wants his people to be led by a person of strong, righteous, character and not a flimsy, wishy-washy person who changes as the culture changes. As we come across the gift of leadership in our Romans passage, we find the word "zeal" immediately after, and this is significant to know!

There were people back in the Bible times who were called Zealots. They were so dedicated to a certain teaching their behavior was extreme and completely counter-cultural. They lived with such dedication that no other person or thing mattered except their teaching. Zeal is also very closely related to the word "passion," which we will get too later in the book. You will discover that passion and zeal go together because they are both decision based actions rather than emotional based responses. When you lead with zeal, you are deciding each day to live according to God's will which is the greatest act of rebellion one can demonstrate. You want to be a rebel? Lead others into a relationship with Jesus! It sounds soft, lame, churchy, boring, and definitely not entertaining. But, when all the gadgets, fun, video games, movies, snapchats, egos, trophies, and success are taken away, the ones left standing with Christ will be the greatest victors of all! They will stand fulfilled. They will stand completely satisfied

> That passion and zeal go together because they are both decision based actions rather than emotional based responses.

and joyous because of the life they led not seeking the approval of man, but by seeking the will of God.

Doing acts of mercy. Have you ever played the game "Mercy" with your friends or siblings? It's where you take each other's hand, interlock the fingers, and start twisting each other's hands as hard as you can until the other person cries out "mercy!" It's really a fun game if you are the person who gets to hear the other bend and cry for you to stop inflicting such pain. One of my best friends, Josiah, and I played this all the time when we were younger. I would always end up beating him, until one day. We played and he destroyed me! To this day he will brag about his dominance in the game Mercy, and bragging rights are rightfully his.

How does all this relate to the spiritual gift of mercy? People with the acts of mercy have a greater sensitivity to those in painful situations and are more motivated to not just "feel bad for them," but get up and actually do something to relieve their pain. You may work in this gift when you hear of opportunities to work at a soup kitchen, collect food for a homeless shelter, hand out blankets to the homeless in your community, support children through programs like Compassion International™, WorldVision™, ASON™, etc. Maybe you sign up for mission trips that have you building clean water sources in 3rd world countries or going around your community raising awareness for girls and boys caught in sex trafficking. However, this gift also plays out in day to day relationships. You may have a friend who is very hard to love. They may push people away, making the relationship difficult. Yet, really, they just need to continually be reminded that they are loved and accepted and that Jesus wants them just as much as He wants you or any other person, no matter how good or bad they are. Not just anyone can love these people the way God desires. That's why he has given this gift to people so that the Gospel would have a name, face, and a consistent message of love and truth streaming into the lives of those in need.

What a spectacular picture we paint when the Church lives out their spiritual gifts! The way we love each other is by living out our gifts in the context of the local church. Instead of trying to "put up with each other" or "get over offenses" in the church, let's focus on the grace given to us to share with others!

We just covered a lot. I want you to PAUSE and express in words, images, or phrases what God is wanting you to remember and put into practice from this chapter. When you are finished, flip over to the next chapter to discover the **mission** we have as the Church.

CHAPTER 10
THE CHURCH: PART 3 – THE MISSION

Our definition of the Church is this: *One Body, united in One Spirit, on mission to share and teach the Gospel to All People.* In the previous chapter we broke down what it means to live as one body, united in One Spirit. Looking forward, we will take a look at what this mission is we have as the Church and what your part is in it.

Take a minute or two, and in the space provided to draw, write, or sketch whatever images pop into your head when you hear the "mission."

Obviously I have no idea what you filled that creative space with, but I am fairly confident there is an association between what you wrote down or drew and what I am about to say: mission is action. The Church has a mission given to us by God. It's a call to action that requires a yes or no response from Christians. Working in full-time youth ministry for 7 years and having worked with students your age now for almost 10 years, I have started to notice a few things concerning the mission you have been given.[18]

When you think, "mission," you have to think, "motivation." When I see students your age so incredibly busy with 10 other activities and struggle to participate in youth group, I ask myself, "What motivates them to do all this stuff and why isn't the motivation the same or greater for God's stuff?" It's a gut-level question everyone needs to ask because, let me tell you something, the **mission is the motivator.** However, if you don't believe God's mission is

---

18 Compared to some youth pastors, I'm still just getting my feet wet in ministry. I know guys who have been serving young people for 27+ years...A huge shout out to you long-term youth pastors, keep up the awesome work!

necessary, you will never be motivated to sign on to the greatest call to action one can ever receive this side of heaven! You will use the excuse of "Oh, someone else is doing that, I don't need to," to get you out of the life saving mission of Jesus! Why would you want out of that? Is it hard? Absolutely! But what isn't these days? I hear of students taking AP classes, and being involved in 3-4 extra curricular activities, slandered by their friends, their homes are hurting and full of pain, and in the midst of all that, the mission to save lives through Jesus is somehow deemed unnecessary and **too difficult.** Maybe our perspective is off. Have we viewed the mission of Christ as something that is to enhance our lives? Or is it about bringing true, life-changing power into the hearts of others? The mission of Jesus is motivating when you focus on the main purpose: **to share and Teach the Gospel to all people.**

When you take the focus off of you, you are able to step back and see the incredible joy that is found in not only sharing the Good News of Jesus with others, but also sitting down and being able to help them understand the Word of God in order to receive the life of God! What does this purpose look like in the life of a 21st century teenager in modern America?

Share the Good News

When it comes to sharing the Good News, I believe you first must ask God to identify the friends He wants you sharing with. This is critical because He knows the hearts of those who are ready to receive the Gospel. You can confidently approach your friends with the Gospel because you know God has been preparing their hearts to receive it. He will do the heart work. He wants you to sow the seed of the Gospel in the already prepared heart! Sharing the Good News starts with prayer and must continue to be covered in prayer. However, when it comes down to it, God isn't going to take over your vocal cords and do the work. You must step out and actually share when the opportunity is given. God will help you identify when the right moment is if you have been praying about it. He will nudge your heart to share, and when you sense that nudge, it's your time to accept the mission and share the Good News. Here's my challenge to you right now, in this moment. **REACH5.** I challenge you to pray and ask God for the names of five friends who need to hear the Gospel of Jesus. Write down their names in the space below. For the next 30 days, pray every day that God would (1) soften their hearts to receive the Gospel and (2) He would give you an opportunity to share the Good News. He will help you. He will give you the exact words you need to say. Jesus reassures his disciples of this truth in Mark 13:11, *"Whenever you are arrested and brought to trial, do not worry beforehand about what to say. Just say whatever is given you at the time, for it is not you speaking, but the Holy Spirit."* You are constantly on trial in the spiritual realm. Every time you see an open door to share the Gospel, Satan will be sitting there, trying to make you cower away in fear, trembling in your loss for words and, greater yet, your fear of losing self-pride and possibly friends. This is why prayer is so critical! Don't enter the battlefield without preparing your heart and asking God to go before you and prepare their hearts! You can enter confidently when you spend time consistently praying. Consistent prayer leads to confident sharing.

Teach the Good News

You have been challenged to share the Good News. Now I am challenging you to teach the Good News. When I say our mission as the Church is to teach the Good News, I am thinking specifically of you and your friends engaging in conversation about the truth of Scripture.

Recently, in our student ministry, I have seen many SRHIGH students step up and be willing to receive the mission of teaching the Good News to their peers. Whether it was during our Friday night outreach, Wednesday night ministry, or on Sunday mornings, they have taken time to pray, work through a Scripture passage, prepare a message and deliver it to their peers. Let's hear from a few students who have been actively teaching God's Word.

"Teaching God's Word at Youth Group has helped me get out of my comfort zone. I would most likely never lead a Bible study by myself, and by being asked to do one puts me in a position to grow as a Christian. I then put myself in a position that God can use me as a light to others. Also, not only will I grow more comfortable leading these studies, but I will feel more comfortable sharing my faith to

others and living my faith out each and every day. In addition to this, leading a Bible study requires preparation. This preparation brings me to look deeper into each verse, allowing me to learn more about what God has to say. No longer do I just read the Word just to read it, but now, even in one simple verse, I can come up with an application to my life that will change the way I live."

-*Shane Striech, Senior at Waseca High School.*

I grew up with my faith spoon-fed to me. Prior to personally getting involved in our youth group 2020 and our Sunday School classes, I had the thought that showing up for church and attending a few church-run camps was more than meeting the "requirements" that all have been given by God. However, after attending some weekend conferences that included service projects, I really became passionate about my faith. I wanted to live a life that was ignited by God's passion and love. With my newfound excitement came a need for a deeper relationship with God. Thankfully, Pastor Zach was there to help guide me, along with everyone else in the youth ministries. I was taught to view the Bible not as a history book, but as a tool that was still relevant today. From the lists of names in the Old Testament, to the miraculous works described in the New Testament, every piece of Scripture was necessary to understand how to live in accordance with God. In Sunday school classes I learned how to break down and understand what God had packed into the Bible. By first looking at the characteristics of God, and then looking at the relationship shown between the people and God, it became easy to understand many different passages in the Bible. This method to understand the Bible was especially reinforced on Wednesday nights at church. As a youth group, we looked at the characteristics of God for one whole year. The theme never changed that year, and as a group we started to see who God really is and what his role in our lives should be.

"By focusing on who God is, reading His word, and understanding His relationship with His people, I am able to take any situation and look at it through God's eyes. Without the encouragement of Pastor Zach, my youth group, and the church body overall, I wouldn't be where I am today. Today, I am a firm believer in Christ,

and I am constantly following the path that He made for me. I have confidently been able to give several messages in the past couple years, and I have also led multiple Bible studies with my peers. Most importantly, however, I have been able to strengthen my personal faith with the help of those around me."

-Ben Stoesz, Senior at Waseca High School.

My vision for you as students is to not just be able to teach the Word inside the four walls of a church, but anywhere you go. You have a set of skills that will allow you to understand God's Word. Have you seen this diagram before? I hope so, it was a few chapters ago. I want to refresh you quickly on this tool.

God. Seek to learn about God's character in any Scripture you read.

Us. Seek to discover how your relationship with God informs who you are as a person.

Transformation. Seek to discover the desired change God wants to bring as a result of encountering Him.

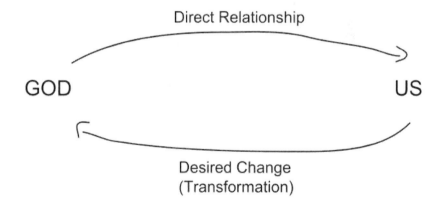

Direct Relationship

GOD   US

Desired Change
(Transformation)

So, take John 1:1-5 and break it down using the tool provided above and the space below. When you're done, feel free to check out the Appendix to see if you are catching on to the concept of this tool.

In my heart, I believe the mission we all have as Christians is to share and teach the message of Jesus to all people. Jesus himself passed along the mission to all of us right before He went up into heaven: *make disciples of all people.* (Matthew 28:19-20). Jesus cares more about the condition of a person's heart than their outward appearance. You have no excuse: If God calls you to love a person with the Gospel, you do it, you just say "YES!"

Just Say Yes

I have a good friend Ron who is roughly 60ish. He helped me buy my first house in Waseca. He has mentored me through many ministry trials, life trials, and he has been a huge supporter of this project RISEUP. Throughout the years I have heard him repeat a phrase that has stuck with me, and I want to pass it on to you. When it comes to the mission of the Church, *Just say, "Yes."* The method he uses a lot of times to get people to help out with a ministry event is by telling people to not think about it and instead, "just say yes." Now, his goal is to get them focused on the mission at hand instead of all the reasons why they shouldn't help. You see, we have a commitment issue within the Church and it needs to be cured. A lot of times it's just a matter of people saying "yes" and deciding to forego all the other things they wanted to do. However, it's also gaining a fresh perspective on the mission the Church has been given. Jossiah, a youth leader at the Christian Family Center in Brooklyn, NY, says the tagline of their church is "Family on a mission." That captures perfectly the essence of the Church; One family on one massive mission to share and teach the Gospel to all people! What is my challenge to you? **Just Say, "Yes."** Christ has called you to share and teach the Gospel of Jesus to all the world, what is your response?

CHAPTER 11
THE PASSION

"All consuming; U structure your life around it." This definition of passion was given by Micah, a senior in high school from Anchorage, Alaska. Micah has grown up in the church. His family is very involved and he himself is a very busy guy. He attends full time post-secondary schooling, works, attends church, and tries to keep a balanced life. Being a solid church student, Micah knows a lot. He knows everything that every good Christian student should know. Yet, Micah shared that he struggled with having a passion for God because of how active and busy his life is. Can you relate at all? I believe it's time we re-adjust our understanding of this word "passion." To do this, we need to point our attention onto someone other than us.

The Passion of Christ (Matthew 26:38-39)

It's a high possibility you have seen the movie, *The Passion of the Christ.* This movie takes liberty to portray the beating and crucifixion of Jesus in the most grotesque, yet real way possible. The passion of Jesus was not glorious, but it brought great glory! The crucifixion of Christ was not popular, but it sparked a movement of followers that were crucified upside down, beheaded, flayed alive by whips and then crucified, crucified in an x shape, speared to death, etc. One of the greatest arguments for the Christian faith is the dedicated, all-consuming passion its followers had. The true definition of passion lies not just in the death of its followers, but in the submission to their God.

If you looked up the word "passion," you would eventually discover that this word comes from the Latin language meaning *"suffer."* When we say we are passionate about something we typically associate it with words like: dedication, motivation, intensity, etc. Yet, we see Jesus passionate to do God's will even when it meant suffering. Really, you could call the movie *"The Suffering of the Christ."* However, this isn't as flashy and cool sounding, right? You are not going to start a Facebook page called "The Suffering Ones" and expect a huge response. Isn't that exactly what Jesus did though? He set the example of passionate obedience to God's will and called people to follow Him. He never asked his followers to "like" what He was teaching. He said, "Follow." You cannot ask people to follow you to where you yourself have not been. Yet, Jesus, before the foundations of the world, knew He would be hanging on a cross, suffering, unto death in submission to His Father and in love for His people. Therefore He was able to call His followers to, *"Pick up your cross and follow after me"* (Mark 8:34).

Jesus calls us to suffer as he suffered. The ultimate purpose of Jesus' suffering was not suffering itself. It led to a glorious resurrection and crowning of Jesus as all-powerful, King of Kings, and Lord of Lords! In this supreme transfer of power the gates to Heaven flung open to all those who confess with their mouth that Jesus is Lord and believe in their hearts God raised Him from the dead (Romans 10:9). Colossians 1:13-14 says it a bit differently, *"He has delivered us from the domain of darkness and transferred us to the kingdom of his Beloved Son, in whom we have redemption, the forgiveness of sins."* In His great submission to God's will, Jesus made the greatest heist in human history. He snatched humans from darkness and brought them into the Kingdom of Heaven!

This is great and all, actually, the greatest news ever proclaimed! Yet, the call to suffer has another layer we need to uncover. It isn't the end, but it is a reality that comes more than once. I believe God gives his people many, many opportunities to show great obedience and give up our will for the will of God, no matter the outcome. I want to focus on one specific opportunity that Jesus had which I believe we all can relate to.

The "How Strong Are You" Test

"Then Jesus was led up by the Spirit into the wilderness to be tempted by the devil." (Matthew 4:1)

Have you been to a county or state fair where they have the game that tests how strong you are? You know, the one where you swing the big hammer as hard as you can and watch to see if you make the little light go all the way to the top? I haven't personally done it, but it sure looks like fun (especially us guys who want to impress our lady friends and show off our huge muscles).

It seems like we, as humans, are constantly being tested. Whether it's in school, at home, with our friends, at church, at our jobs, or playing in the backyard, there is always a dynamic of "how strong are you?" Let's use test taking as an example. I'm horrible at taking tests. Yeah, I made it through school, but whenever it came to test taking, I wasn't the guy to cheat off of if you wanted a good grade. Yet, I knew plenty of those people who were the "cheat worthy" type. They barely studied and they walked in on the day of the test and spent what seemed like five minutes and put their pencil down just as I was barely getting my name down. I mean, come on! Why did they get all the test taking brain power? Before I get too wild and crazy on our awesome test taking friends, we have to remember that when you see a God-allowed weakness there's always a God-given strength. For me, it is paper writing. Test-taking always challenged me, but paper writing, now THAT I can do. For seminary work we would be constantly writing huge papers and I would bang them out in an afternoon - no problem.

You see, it's in our natural world to test and be tested. This is nothing new. We see the testing or temptation of Jesus and it reminds us that, even though Jesus was God, He underwent difficult temptations that tested His spiritual ability to obey God. He was tested because he was in the flesh. What do I mean by "flesh?" The flesh does not just refer to our physical body, but our natural desire to pervert and corrupt the righteous (or right) ways that God has laid out for us. For Jesus, God's right plan was to have Him to be the perfect substitution for our incomplete, incapable, lack of spiritual righteousness. Even though Jesus was fully God while He was fully man, He was still in the flesh, He battled to not pervert the ways of God. Please hear me: **Jesus never perverted the ways of God, not even one time.** He was tempted. Satan made it really difficult for Jesus, but Jesus never acted to please his flesh. Even after three temptations, each targeting different areas of Christ's humanity, Jesus remained perfect. Let's take a closer look at the testing of Christ's obedience to God's Will. The three areas of Christ's tested humanity were: *sufficiency, faith* and *power.*

Test #1: Sufficiency (Matthew 4:1-3). Okay, first, when was the last time you fasted at least 24 hours? Now go 40 days with no food, only to have someone come along and say, "You have fasted forty days and it's time to have a little food. Come on, you've been a good Christian, you deserve it." What is the line of deceit? Satan has made you think that because you did something "good" you somehow deserve a break. The truth is, you do deserve food, but you don't eat based on your "good deed," you eat when God decides it's time. You see, Satan was going after the human inclination to rely on self rather than God. The word used to describe this is "sufficiency." Sufficiency questions, "Who do you rely on to provide for you?" Satan was attacking the human weakness to be "self-sufficient" rather than "God-sufficient." He knew Jesus could turn those rocks into bread (probably really tasty bread, too). Yet Jesus was able to find His way out. What was His way out? The greater question is, how did he understand he was being tempted?

"Jesus answered, 'It is written: Man should not live on bread alone, but on every word that comes from the mouth of God.'" (Matthew 4:4)

If you are reading this, then you struggle with being tempted to pervert or corrupt the right ways of God. I'm not calling you a terrible sinful person, but it's just the facts, we are inclined as humans to struggle with obeying the right ways of God. So how do we, as Jesus did, identify the deceitful ways of Satan? The very Word of God. Jesus is actually quoting from the book of Deuteronomy (the fifth book of the Torah, or the Law of Moses). Deuteronomy 8:3 says this:

"And he humbled you and let you hunger and fed you with manna, which you did not know, nor did your fathers know, that he might make you know that man does not live by bread alone, but man lives by every word that comes from the mouth of the LORD."

Jesus was able to decipher the lie of Satan with the filter of God's

Word. Consider this, if you want to be able to identify a fake $20 bill you study the real thing so well that when a fake one comes across you can spot a fake. You have to understand that Jesus didn't come in the form of a baby and instantly know the whole Old Testament Scriptures. He grew up a child just like we did. He studied the law, He memorized it, and He made sure He knew exactly what it said. Luke 2:52 states this about the boy Jesus, *"Jesus increased in wisdom and in stature and in favor with God and man."*

Just because you grew up in the church, with Christian parents or with Christian friends, doesn't mean anything unless YOU decide to study God's Word and allow God to transform your life. Like Ben shared earlier, it wasn't until he decided for himself that it was time to get serious about his faith that he actually started to grow and become passionate about God! Jesus was God in flesh, yet he studied, grew, and developed. If Jesus studied God's Word it's pretty safe to say we too need to study God's Word to identify and overcome temptation as well. Do you want to defeat temptation? You will need to find your sufficiency in the Word and Power of God.

Test #2: "Don't test God" (Matthew 4:5-6).

"He will command his angels concerning you, and they will lift you up in their hands, so that you will not strike your foot against a stone."

You see what Satan did there? Re-read it and look for something peculiar about WHAT Satan used to tempt Jesus. (Stop, don't check your Twitter feed, keep focused on the task at hand:). Did you find it? Satan used the very words of God to tempt Jesus into testing God. Was Jesus going to really believe that God would come through on his promise and rescue Him? If He did believe, he should jump off and prove His faith to Satan. However, in doing so, that would have broken a more important command as stated in Deuteronomy 6:16 which says, *"You shall not put the Lord your God to the test, as you tested him in Massah."* Jesus knows this command and quotes it right after Satan gets done laying out the temptation. Jesus didn't just know the Scripture and the command, He had it working powerfully in His heart so when it came time to test God, to break the command given in Scripture, He remained faithful to the Word of God and overcame the temptation.

This is why Satan is called the great deceiver and father of lies. He even twists the Word of God to make us believe we are doing something right when, in reality, we may be disobeying God. It is so critical that you don't just know what the verses say, but why God has given them for you to follow. Remember, Scripture is used to accomplish God's great purpose of saving lost souls and making saved souls become more like Christ. Christ set the example of discernment when Scripture was being used to tempt Him to disobey God. If you find yourself in a situation where Scripture seems to be saying something contradictory to the Gospel, it's probably Satan twisting it. Every ink stroke in that book is designed to clarify Jesus and help people live in the power of Jesus. If you find a verse leading you to something that would make Jesus confusing or weaken your ability to passionately spread the Gospel, it's not of God but a twisting of Scripture. Scripture will always point you to God and to living in His right ways.

Test #3: False worship (Matthew 4:8-11).

"Then the devil took him to the holy city and had him stand on the highest point of the temple. 'If you are the Son of God,' he said, 'throw yourself down. For it is written: 'He will command his angels concerning you, and they will lift you up in their hands, so that you will not strike your foot against a stone.'"

Now, you may be asking yourself, "How does Satan have authority to give Jesus (God) the kingdoms of the world?" That is a great question! Check out this passage:

"And he said to him, 'As for you, you were dead in your transgressions and sins, in which you used to live when you followed the ways of this world and of the ruler of the kingdom of the air, the spirit who is not at work in those who are disobedient." (Ephesians 2:1-2)

You see, to a certain degree, God has allowed Satan to rule the earth and set up a *"dominion of darkness"* as Colossians 1:13 states.

In this temptation of Jesus there is a recognition of power Satan possesses. Satan recognizes the power that has been given to him by God but in a very twisted way. He acts like Jesus "forgets" about this "power allowance" and starts off his temptation by promising something that he in fact was never given. Satan presents things as he wants us to see, not as they really are. Jesus was tempted to see Satan as one able to give all this power away when really, all Satan wanted was another person to worship him and reject God. In other words, Satan wanted another false-worshiper.

How did Jesus discern and reject the empty lie Satan presented? Again, Jesus quotes Scripture that was not just buried in his mind, but had also taken root in His heart.

"Jesus said to him, 'Away from me, Satan! For it is written: 'Worship the Lord your God, and serve him only." (Matthew 4:10)

Not only did Jesus quote Scripture, he commands Satan WITH Scripture. Jesus demonstrates once again the power of God's Word living inside us. It gives us authority to not just "resist the devil" (James 3:7) but command him away as Jesus does here in Matthew 4. The temptation to fall down on our knees before anybody BUT God can be commanded away by quoting Scripture when that temptation comes.

Scripture says that Jesus was led up by the Spirit into the wilderness to be tempted by the devil. Now, let's be clear on something, ***"Jesus was led up by the Spirit."*** This testing was not an accident. God led Jesus into the wilderness where He knew temptation would occur. He knew the flesh of Jesus would be tested to see if He would pervert and corrupt the way God had ordained Him to walk in. God did not tempt Jesus and God never tempts us. Jesus was led up by the Spirit and then Satan came along and did the tempting. It's almost like Satan and God have this unspoken agreement that God will allow a certain level of temptation from Satan. Again, though, let Scripture inform your understanding of temptation.

"No temptation has overtaken you except what is common to mankind. And God is faithful; he will not let you be tempted beyond what you can bear. But when you are tempted, he will also provide a way out so that you can endure it." (1 Corinthians 10:13)

You see, Jesus was under the influence of Satan but God remained in control. He provided a way out. He didn't lead Jesus into the dessert without an escape plan, and He will never allow you to be tempted without an escape plan. God's escape plan for you is His Alive Word. We must know it, study it, and embed it in our hearts so when temptation does come, we can pass the test and submit to God's will!

I want you to PAUSE and think about what it means to command temptation away. Do this for me: in the space provided below, draw/ write out what comes to your mind when you hear the word "resist." What does this word mean to you? What do you think of?

Then, I want you to write out Deuteronomy 6:13 on the same page in a prayer to God asking Him to help you command temptation away in the name of Jesus Christ.

"How's Your Vision?"

About a year ago, I started to have some eye-sight problems. After I would put my son to bed, I would walk out of his dark room into our kitchen where the lights were all on. I would start squinting right away because my eyes just couldn't handle it! Well, after months of this going on, I decided it was time to have the old eyeballs examined. I went in and discovered I had a case of "dormant far-sightedness." What does this mean? Well, to be far-sighted means you need help seeing things up close. Why is this the case? For me, I went through four years of seminary (aka: LOTS OF READING and typing papers). And, as a youth pastor, I work every day on my computer, typing messages, emailing, designing stuff, etc. My eyes had been forced to focus on things up close for so long they actually started to weaken. It was just recently (after all those years) that this dormant far-sightedness decided it was time to reveal it needed a little help. I gave my eyeballs what they wanted - glasses. I tell you what, it's so much better working on the computer and reading. My eyes aren't strained and I can work longer and more efficiently. My vision needed some help to be effective.

Our spiritual vision needs some help too. This is what Michael Baker, a High School Pastor at Highlands Church in Scottsdale, AZ says about passion, *"[Passion is a] consuming factor for your actions. It's the lens from which you love and see everything through."* I love this definition of passion because it's dead on. The passion Jesus has for us needs to be the lens through which we love and see everything and everybody through. We love people like Christ because Christ has spilled His passion into our lives! Our motivation to live out the mission of Jesus is fueled by our awe-inspiring, humble response to the passion Jesus showed on our behalf. When we have claimed to follow Jesus, His power of sacrifice and His overcoming of temptation resides in our hearts. We remain faithful, not because of our great ability to be faithful, but because the faithfulness of Jesus residing within us. Our faith rests in the life of Jesus inside of us. Our power to live passionately and sacrificially comes from the life of Jesus (Galatians 2:20).

To wrap this up, I want you to take a few minutes to consider this passage of scripture:

Then he said to them, "My soul is overwhelmed with sorrow to the point of death. Stay here and keep watch with me." Going a little farther, he fell with his face to the ground and prayed, "My Father, if it is possible, may this cup be taken from me. Yet not as I will, but as you will." Then he returned to his disciples and found them sleeping. "Couldn't you men keep watch with me for one hour?" he asked Peter. "Watch and pray so that you will not fall into temptation. The spirit is willing, but the flesh is weak." He went away a second time and prayed, "My Father, if it is not possible for this cup to be taken away unless I drink it, may your will be done. (Matthew 26:38-42)

Living passionately for Jesus is not easy at all. Jesus prayed multiple times to walk a different road than submission to His Father's will. Yet, even in the depths of His sorrow and pain, He surrenders, He chooses to suffer. That is passion.

PAUSE to consider these questions as you think about the suffering of Jesus on your behalf and those around you.

1. Ask Jesus what He thinks about you. Write down whatever comes to mind.

_____

_____

_____

_____

2. Jesus passionately loves you. He showed that on the cross. How have you experienced this love in your daily life?

_____

_____

_____

_____

3. What areas of your life is God calling you to live passionately, and possibly to receive humiliation and rejection? What steps will you take right away to start living passionately for the Gospel?

_____

_____

_____

_____

CHAPTER 12
THE BEGINNING

As you near the end of this book, I want to say congrats and thank for you taking valuable time to invest in having God challenge you in your passion to live on mission for the Gospel! To wrap up this journey, I want to do two things with you before we go: (1) *Reveal our hunger for God's will* and (2) *Discover some things that are holding you up from seeing your passion revived so you can live out your mission!*

There's a great story of Jesus in the Gospel of John that I want us to look at as we seek to have God reveal our spiritual hunger for him. What's awesome about the book of John is that we get to experience the person of Jesus so much more than any other book of the Bible. We see a lot of His miracles, including His first miracle that no other Gospel records. The greatest part of John's Gospel is the very clear picture we see of the crazy close relationship Jesus has with His Father. Let's check out John 4:31-34 to see more of Jesus in action.

"Meanwhile his disciples urged him, 'Rabbi, eat something." But he said to them, 'I have food to eat that you know nothing about.' Then his disciples said to each other, 'Could someone have brought him food?' My food,' said Jesus, 'is to do the will of him who sent me and to finish his work."

Jesus is interacting with His disciples about food. Instead of dropping to their level, He takes them to Theology 101. Here is a short entry from my journal reflections that I believe help capture what Jesus was doing with his disciples.

"Doing the will of God is so satisfying! Jesus makes it clear that

fulfilling God's purposes satisfied the greatest hunger all humans experience, that of purpose and calling."

Jesus knew the will of the Father was to have the Gospel unify all people in purpose of glorifying God. That meant stepping across socially heated boundaries (Jews and Samaritans hated each other) and extend the truth of God to a Samaritan woman who desperately needed the message of Jesus. I believe the bigger lesson Jesus was trying to get His disciples to understand is that doing the will of God creates the greatest hunger pain while delivering the greatest feeling of satisfaction. The disciples were worried about Jesus' physical hunger while Jesus was concerned about their spiritual hunger.

Friends, I am concerned about our spiritual hunger. Here is the rest of my journal entry to hopefully allow you to see the struggle this is for every person who has a faith in Jesus.

"How satisfied do I find myself when it comes to serving God? Am I consumer of the good things of God or a servant of God? A servant finds joy in their work/blessings while a consumer is never satisfied, always wanting more, struggling to nurture a spirit of thankfulness. The woman at the well started off as a consumer, wanting the good things of God but in the end, we never really discover if the woman truly became a servant of Jesus. The point is, God wants me living as a satisfied servant doing His will and not a consumer of the good things of God."

I believe our level of satisfaction directly relates to our level of hunger. The more we are satisfied in our mission as a servant of God the more we will hunger to serve him. If our hunger to serve is hardly noticeable, I'm not sure how satisfied we are in being His servant.

Finding purpose and satisfaction in doing God's will is difficult. It's difficult because the minute you put down this book and think about what changes God wants to make in your life you're instantly going to hit the wall of reality; the wall built up by so many things that hinder your ability to live with a revived passion for the Gospel.

I want you to PAUSE here and consider, *"How much do I find myself wanting to serve God's Will? On a consistent basis, do I think more about serving God or serving myself?"* Go ahead and journal your thoughts below.

Hindrances

Alright. If we are wanting to serve God, doing His will, there are some things I believe that can be great hindrances if not properly addressed in our life. I have only included two main ones that seem to rise to the surface as I interviewed many different youth pastors, parents, and entertainment.

Parents. I believe your parents have a significant role in the development of your faith. If they are not living out their role, they are being a barrier that God needs to work on. Now, I want you to do three things for me here: (1) read this section with open ears and heart, (2) get your parents to read this section with open ears and heart, and (3) discuss what you read with open ears and heart so together you can grow in your passion for the Gospel.

Being a youth pastor, I have learned that my role is not to be the primary shaper of a student's faith, but to be a supplemental piece of support for the parents of students who are plugged into my ministry. As I met with youth pastors across the country I heard time and time again comments like the following. *"There is a low percentage of parents living like Christ,"* (Darin Brown, Associate Pastor at Harvest Community Church in Selah, Washington) and, *"Parents are not modeling church involvement for kids"* (Pastor Patrick from Northside Church in Baldwin, NY). There is a critical role parents play in the development of a student's faith and it cannot be overlooked or passed off to the student ministry of a church. How can parents start setting a better example of what it looks like to live with a revived passion and on mission for the Gospel?

Priorities. Dave, a youth pastor from the Chicago, IL, says, *"Priorities need to be set by parents."* A priority communicates purpose. When your student is going off to school at 6am in the morning and not returning until 9pm at night, what is the purpose for that schedule? To be very frank, as Nate Stenholz, a youth pastor from Wisconsin put it, *"The American Dream, school, sports, etc. are more important than God."* When you as parents allow your students to be consumed in the flurry of school activities, you are silently re-affirming the lie that all those things are more important than God. I realize everyone who reads this book has a different experience with school schedules but I don't think it's uncommon to see students being at school fairly early in the morning and not getting back until later in the evening with a few hours of homework every night, only to repeat the same cycle daily for nine months. When students are exhausted from their school schedule, what energy do they have left for God? Spending time with the Lord requires focus, it requires energy. Yet, all that energy and focus has been taken up by all the other activities in the student's schedule. Camryn, an 11th grader from Scottsdale, AZ, said this about the impact of school on a student's spiritual life, *"High school hinders you, it's a busy life. It happened to me my freshman year. I was doing the "right things" but it wasn't enough until I got involved in small groups and surrounded myself with people of similar passion."*

Whether JR or SR High, life is busy when we let it happen to us. However like Camryn, you too need to make some purposeful decisions to start prioritizing your life around Jesus' stuff. Instead of filling your schedules up with the busyness of sports, drama team, 4-H, FFA, Science Olympiad, etc., make sure you are, as Camryn so awesomely put it, *"Gettin' busy with Jesus."* I'm not saying you decide to completely drop all your activities, but prioritize your schedule with the purpose of having the energy and awareness to share and teach the Gospel to those you come in contact with every day.

So, how do you re-prioritize your life and get busy with Jesus? Remember, priority means purpose. You live with intention. Here's where to start:

Evaluate your spiritual gifts. Re-read the section on spiritual gifts we went over previously. Pray and talk with your parents, your youth pastor/youth leader, and Christian friends about what spiritual gifts they see in you. Identify a few of your gifts, and then…

Evaluate the activities you are currently involved with. Remember, spiritual gifts are not JUST for serving inside the church. If you are a Christian, you are part of the Church which exists anywhere a Spirit-filled believer is present. So, wherever you go, you represent the Church, the body of Christ. Christ gives us a mission to share and teach the Gospel and He equips us to live it out! When you are at track practice running, how are you able to utilize your gifts? When you are practicing your lines for the school play, how is God wanting you to share and teach the Gospel with your drama team? If you are on the basketball team and your spiritual gift is teaching, how do those go together? Your spiritual gifts are meant to foster spiritual fruit. In any of those situations, I believe you constantly need to have the outlook of "spiritual steps." What steps can you help your friends make toward believing in the Gospel? One day it may be just talking about your team or activity, and the next day it could be sharing something you are struggling with and how your faith in Christ has helped you. Before you know it, the Holy Spirit will have used you to walk your friend step by step into the arms of Christ!

Intentionally limit yourself. We live in an unlimited world. Any cell phone company nowadays provides unlimited everything. We don't like boundaries and sadly enough that attitude has infiltrated our homes and our spiritual lives. If you want to be a student living with passion for Jesus Christ, you must joyfully live within limitations. Let's look at this passage from Philippians 2:5-8 to see a perfect example of living within limitations,

"Have this mind among yourselves, which is yours in Christ Jesus, who, though he was in the form of God, did not count equality with God a thing to be grasped, but emptied himself, by taking the form of a servant, being born in the likeness of men. And being found in human form, he humbled himself by becoming obedient to the point of death, even death on a cross."

Earlier in the book I made a reference to Jesus "cloaking" His God-nature. In deciding to cover up His God-nature, He willingly put Himself under human limitation. We know Christ did not do this with a bad attitude and begrudgingly but joyfully (Hebrews 12:2). God desires us to joyfully live within limitation. In reflecting Christ we are able to focus on helping our friends take those spiritual steps towards Christ. When we are living insanely busy, we have no time for intentional, meaningful, Gospel-saturated conversations. Live limited and see what God will do!

Continual Conversation. Is there continual conversation in your home about the Good News of Jesus? If you want your students living passionately for Jesus, you must be blazing the path they walk in! Do you have a consistent time with the Lord that you are able to then share about with your kids? Notice, I didn't say you have to have "family devotions." I realize your schedules are crazy and hectic and it's hard to even see each other sometimes. Yet, can you as parents intentionally set aside time in the crazy lives you live to meet with God? The more vibrant your faith is the more motivating it will be to share with them!

In these days of texting, I would make a safe guess that you have some sort of texting experience. Would you commit to sending a verse every day to your student? Would you commit to sharing through text or when you see them at home how God is working in your life and how God wants to work in theirs?

Taylor Wilson, a former youth director and now staff member at Lord of Life Lutheran Church in Maple Grove, MN, says he believes strongly that, *"Historically, around the age of Martin Luther, the role of the family was for shaping student's expectations of prayer and spiritual growth. Now, parents don't feel as confident in teaching their kids."* I believe we have seen parents lose confidence in teaching their students. Do you feel this way?

Take heart, you are not alone. This is a huge responsibility, but one that you are not alone in. My prayer is that the youth ministry your students are involved with is designed to reach out to you as well and equip you. Ask for names of parents whom you can connect with. Network yourself with other parents!

Most importantly though, make a commitment to pursue Jesus more passionately each day. Make the sacrifice in scheduling so that God has the best time of your day. Set that example for your students because they are watching, they are observing, they are waiting to see adults consistently blazing the path of passionate living because they are tired of trying to figure it out on their own. Set the example, watch and see what happens!

Okay, parents, if you made it to the end, thank you! Please feel free to photocopy this section if you need to review it and take notes. But for now, we press on into the second thing I believe is hindering our students from living passionately for Jesus.

Entertainment. While I wrote this book, I got distracted by Facebook, Twitter, and other media sources. By the time you finished reading this book, you probably checked your phone hundreds of times. Why? **We love to be entertained.** Here's the issue, as Will Peterson, High School Intern at Grace Community Church in Los Angeles, CA says, "*Students have an attitude that basically says, 'I would rather entertain myself than serve the Lord and people.*" I am in complete agreement with Will. The more we gorge ourselves on entertainment, the more we fall in love with the message it is sending us: *I am here to make your life happy.* We can't say we want a passionate relationship with Jesus and yet be worshipping the god of entertainment. You will serve one and hate the other, you cannot love both! God is calling you to sacrifice and surrender to His will, which may mean uncomfortable living. You may not feel happy or entertained all the time. However I can guarantee you that whatever God has you doing, you will find a deep satisfaction that entertainment could only dream of providing. I have nothing against movies, music, television, or social media. I enjoy watching shows, listening to music, and seeing the latest movies. The question I am asking you to consider is this: *How much do I engage and what do I engage?*

How much do I engage? I'm going to make this short and sweet: Do you spend less, equal or more time with God than you do with entertainment in your life? I care about you knowing that God, Creator of all, wants a passionate, crazy close relationship with you and the god of entertainment needs to be crushed! So, how much do you engage entertainment in comparison to God? I want you to be honest with yourself and God so He can show you the balance you need to strike. When you get a sense of what you need to cut out, DO IT! Make the sacrifice, suffer a little, it really pays off!

What do I engage? Entertainment is telling you to please yourself. If we are wanting to be vessels that spread the Good News of Christ, we can't be compromising on what we allow into our hearts and minds.

You need to determine now the lines you will not cross when it comes to media engagement. Will you listen to music that communicates anger, sexual content, and swearing, just because it "pumps you up?" Will you watch movies like *The Neighbors* that delivers humorous jokes but is bombarded with vulgarity and sexuality? What line will you not cross for the sake of pleasing yourself? On the flip side of all of that, you have to ask the question, *who will you seek to please?* Not only does that crap dampen our spiritual zeal for living obediently, but it sends a message of hypocrisy and lies to the people around us. We cannot constantly engage in the garbage dumps of entertainment and expect people to believe we love God and want them to love God! You must decide for yourself, is God worth the sacrifice of some humorous laughs and cutting edge thrill rides?

These are just two barriers to spiritual growth that surfaced as I met with students and pastors around the country. There are so many more that could be addressed. I pray you take time to ask God what things in your life are killing your passion. Deal with them! Don't just brush over them as "well they are a normal part of my life." They are smothering your ability to sacrifice for Jesus and see others come to know him!

PAUSE now to ask God for a few things:

1. Ask him what area of entertainment He needs to crush in your life. Write or draw out what He tells you.

2. Ask him to give you a desire to have more conversations about the Bible and the Gospel with your parents. It's a hard job to lead spiritually, pray for your parents!

FINAL THOUGHTS

To wrap-up this journey, I want you to hear more from some of the voices that spoke into the shaping of this book. I want to end with two thoughts from a few people that I believe capture the essence of our mission and equip you with a final perspective to RISEUP.

The first thought has to do with **knowledge.** Check out what Lynnea, a recent graduate who lives in Anchorage, AK, says about her faith, *"When all the knowledge became a practice, my faith became my own."* You see, this whole book could either be another source of knowledge or a tool to help you turn your knowledge into a practice. My prayer is that you take what you have read and turn it into a practice, a daily rhythm of action that starts defining your life by Gospel living. You see, the message of the Gospel is not just a message steeped in the history of Jesus Christ, but as Joe, a Chicago area youth pastor puts it, *"A daily message that needs to be preached and believed in."* The more you practice it, the more your heart experiences its truth, and the more you believe it. It's called a process of transformation and it's one that starts with Christ and ends with Christ. I ask that you seek out God for the steps He wants you to take to transform this knowledge into a practice of believing and living on mission for the Gospel.

The final word I want to share comes from the words of Alejandro. Alejandro is a 9th grade guy who has personally come to know the incredible grace of God and has believed that God is worthy of our time and should be our top priority. When asked how to make God your top priority he responded, *"Spreading the Gospel through your actions."* That, my friends, is what it means to RISEUP. You live your life as a sacrifice for seeing others come to experience the life-giving message of the Gospel. When we find ourselves living that life, we find ourselves living out the true purpose of our lives; to glorify God by living passionately on mission for the Gospel.

WHAT NEXT?

You're done. But now what?

We encourage you to check out our website to discover the next steps you can take with others just like you who are actively seeking God to revive their passion and live their mission!

www.riseupalive.com

Don't forget to follow "riseupalive" on…
Facebook
Twitter
Instagram

RISEUP

APPENDIX

John 1:1-5

Direct Relationship

The Word (v1)   In the beginning (v2)
Life/Light to   Made all things (v3)
all men (v4)   Overcomer of darkness (v5)

GOD   US

God wants us to recognize we are
created beings, who live in darkness
apart from Christ, and who is our only
true life and light!

Desired Change
(Transformation)

BIBLIOGRAPHY

"7 Natural Phenomenons You've Never Seen." Oddee.com. November 06, 2007. oddee.com/item_91568.aspx

"Archaeologists Say They've Uncovered the Site Where Jesus Was Tried.." Accessed January 7, 2015. http://www.relevantmagazine.com/slices/archaeologists-say-theyve-uncovered-site-where-jesus-was-tried

"Artifact Confirms Ancient Bethlehem." N.p., n.d. Web. 15 Aug. 2014. http://www.icr.org/article/6891/310/

"A Tale of Two Fathers.." Accessed October 21, 2014. http://www.pewsocialtrends.org/2011/06/15/a-tale-of-two-fathers/.

"Bible Gt (Great Treasures).." Accessed November 1, 2014. http://greattreasures.org/gnt/main.do

Folger, Tim. "Science's Alternative to an Intelligent Creator: The Multiverse Theory." DiscoverMagazine, December 2008. Accessed March 14, 2014. http://discovermagazine.com/2008/dec/10-sciences-alternative-to-an-intelligent-creator#.UyN2gdy1TfA.

"Heart Facts." Accessed August 15th, 2014. http://upbeatheartsupport.org.uk/medical_matters/heart_facts.html

Horton, Michael. Christless Christianity: the Alternative Gospel of the American Church by Michael Horton (Jun 1 2012). Ada, MI: Baker Books, 1001.

"Martydom Quotes from Christian History." N.p., n.d. Web. 15 Aug. 2014. http://www.christian-history.org/martyrdom-quotes.html

"Nervous System." Accessed September 19th, 2014.
http://www.innerbody.com/image/nervov.html#full-description

"Short Inspirational Student Leadership Quotes.." Accessed
November 3, 2014. http://studentleadership.com/short-
inspirational-quotes/

"The Bible Unearthed." Accessed January 29, 2015.
https://www.nytimes.com/books/first/f/finkelstein-bible.html

"Tacitus: Annals Book 15." Accessed November 3rd, 2014.
http://www.sacred-texts.com/cla/tac/a15040.htm